The Audience Experience

The Audience Experience
A critical analysis of audiences in the performing arts

Jennifer Radbourne, Hilary Glow and Katya Johanson

intellect Bristol, UK / Chicago, USA

First published in the UK in 2013 by
Intellect, The Mill, Parnall Road, Fishponds, Bristol, BS16 3JG, UK

First published in the USA in 2013 by
Intellect, The University of Chicago Press, 1427 E. 60th Street,
Chicago, IL 60637, USA

A catalogue record for this book is available from the
British Library.

Cover designer: Ellen Thomas
Copy-editor: MPS Technologies
Production manager: Melanie Marshall
Typesetting: Planman Technologies

ISBN: 978-1-84150-713-2
EISBN: 978-1-84150-778-1

Printed and bound by Hobbs the Printers Ltd, UK

Contents

Acknowledgements

This book represents the thinking of an international community of scholars with a passion for new research on new performing arts audiences, and we are grateful to the authors for their participation in this initiative. The editing of this collection would not have been possible without the support of the Centre for Memory, Imagination and Invention at Deakin University and Arts Victoria. Thanks in particular to Judy Morton for her ongoing participation and enthusiasm for the research project. We also express our gratitude to research assistants Emma Price and Janet Armstrong. Thanks also to Melanie Marshall at Intellect and Kevin Radbourne for being a generous host.

Contributors

Martin Barker is Emeritus Professor of Film Studies at Aberystwyth University, UK. For the last three years he has been working on the growing phenomenon of streamed live performances into cinemas, including providing a report on audience responses to Picturehouse Cinemas, London.

Lisa Baxter is a UK-based qualitative researcher, brand strategist, ideas consultant and trainer. Her company, The Experience Business, is a strategic insight consultancy that helps arts and cultural organizations meet the needs of 21st century audiences through Strategic Value Creation.

Alan Brown, principal of WolfBrown USA, is a leading researcher and management consultant in the arts and culture sector worldwide. His work focuses on understanding consumer demand for cultural experiences and on helping cultural institutions, foundations and agencies to see new opportunities, make informed decisions and respond to changing conditions.

Elizabeth Carnegie is Programme Director for Creative and Cultural Industries Management at the University of Sheffield, UK. Her research interrogates the role of museums and World Heritage Sites in representing and reflecting cultures and communities.

Brenda Dervin is Professor of Communication and Joan N. Huber Fellow in Social and Behavioral Sciences at Ohio State University, USA. She is most widely known for the 35-year development of her Sense-Making Methodology (SMM) designed to study and research audiences in audience-oriented communicative ways and for designing system interfaces that respond better to audiences and users.

Lois Foreman-Wernet is Associate Professor of Communication at Capital University, Columbus, USA. Her research interests focus on audience-centred approaches to institutional communication, with a particular emphasis on the use of Dervin's Sense-Making Methodology in the study of arts and cultural audiences.

Hilary Glow is Associate Professor and Director of the Arts and Entertainment Management Programme at Deakin University, Australia. Her research addresses arts participation and the management and policy settings that frame the operations and sustainability of cultural organizations.

Katya Johanson is Senior Lecturer in the School of Communication and Creative Arts at Deakin University, Australia. Her research focuses on cultural policy at a federal, state and local level, and particularly on policies that aim to increase public participation in the arts.

Daragh O'Reilly is a Lecturer in Marketing at the University of Sheffield, UK. His primary interest is in the relationships between markets, consumption and culture. This translates into ongoing work in the areas of arts marketing and consumption, the creative imagination, popular music and cultural branding.

Stephanie Pitts is a Reader in Music at the University of Sheffield, UK. Her publications include *Valuing Musical Participation* (Ashgate, 2005) and the recently completed project on musical life histories, *Chances and Choices: Exploring the Impact of Music Education* (OUP, 2012).

Jennifer Radbourne is Emeritus Professor and former Dean of the Faculty of Arts and Education at Deakin University, Australia. Her research and consultancy in arts marketing, arts governance and business development in the creative industries has been published in international journals, books and conference proceedings.

Matthew Reason is Reader in Theatre and Head of Programme for MA Studies in Creative Practice at York St John University, UK. His work explores themes relating to performance documentation, reflective practice, audience research, theatre for young audiences, live art and contemporary performance and cultural policy.

Kim Vincs is Professor in the School of Communication and Creative Arts at Deakin University, Australia, where she is also the is the Director of the Deakin Motion.Lab, Deakin University's motion capture studio and research centre. She is a choreographer, researcher and interactive dance artist who develops new ways of investigating and creating dance using digital technology.

Introduction

Jennifer Radbourne, Hilary Glow and Katya Johanson

What I love about audiences in the theatre is that collective surge that can sometimes happen. It's not always palpable but there's a sense of everyone moving forward, or of relief, or maybe of being uncomfortable, or feeling the person next to you, reacting. It's a reflection of the emotional character of what's going on.

(KAGE Focus Group 2011)

Audiences describe their experience at performances in emotional terms. The above quotation and other similar insights from researchers' conversations with audience members at performances reflect the phenomenon that has shaped the research in this book. The audience and performer crave a connectedness so that creativity is shared. Each audience member attributes the experience with a measure of quality that is entirely personal, based on their own intrinsic needs and their quest for authenticity and spiritual value.

It is this experience that forms the basis of this book as we profile values, benefits, definitions and the means of capturing the dimensions of the experience. For many audience members, the experience is unexpected and uninhibited:

Somehow when you're in the theatre with the cast and in the moment, you're part of it, you're involved and you're emotionally engaged.

(Victorian Opera Focus Group 2011)

For others, it represents a need to self-actualize through the arts experience. But all audiences can describe in quite powerful ways the impact of a 'flow' moment, or a long and compelling engagement with an artist or an arts company. For example:

When you go to a live performance, it's happening, it's in the zone, it's transcendent. You feel like you're a part of something special: you've actually been present, you've borne witness to something.

(Australian Art Orchestra Focus Group 2011)

While audiences are becoming increasingly articulate about what happens to them in the theatre, arts organizations can struggle to identify ways of enhancing this experience. This should come as no surprise in a sector where many of the practitioners have trouble articulating what audiences get out of the experience of attending their work. In the course of conducting research into a number of performing arts companies, we found that while many artistic directors and general managers could discuss their audiences' demographic – the gender, age, postcode, and other subscriber habits – they knew strangely little about what audiences were getting out of the experience. So, despite the great investment of the last twenty years in developing strategic marketing knowhow, we do not know enough about – and do not know how to describe – the benefits that audiences derive from arts experiences. As Alan Brown and Jennifer Novak point out: 'Many who work in the arts, including those of us who do so because of our belief in the transformative power of art, lack a vernacular for communicating its impacts' (Brown & Novak 2007: 5).

This book proposes that it is time for a new kind of audience research which addresses the question: what are audiences thinking, feeling and doing as a product of their engagement with arts practices? The psychologist Daniel Kahneman (2010) draws a distinction between the 'experiencing self' living in the present, and the 'remembering self' which creates and recalls stories of the experiences of the experiencing self. According to Kahneman there is a difference between the experience itself and our recollection of it. When we talk about audience engagement, we talk about audiences that are engaged in *both* experiencing and remembering. Audiences go to the theatre to be engaged in the experience of the moment and in the subsequent recollections of it. The research presented in this book is premised on the notion that there is value in eliciting the audience's reflections on their current and previous arts experiences in order to identify the qualities that build creative engagement, self-expression, self-actualization, and loyalty amongst attenders.

Eliciting such stories is no easy task; as Stephanie Pitts points out in her analysis of audiences for the performance of live music, for audience members to articulate the value of their experience is often 'a challenge since part of its appeal lies in the wordlessness with which it connects participants more deeply with themselves and other people' (Pitts 2005: 10).

The authors included in this book share an interest in audience research. Each contribution is based on the authors' reflections on the intrinsic value of cultural engagement, the question of how to theorize the audience, and how to gather meaningful qualitative data about the audience experience. Taken together these essays make a contribution to new thinking about audience engagement in the arts.

We begin (in Chapter 1) by defining the audience experience and proposing a tool for measuring audience engagement. In addressing this issue, the authors acknowledge that arts audience engagement is central to the artistic mission of most arts institutions and that the aim of measuring the audience or visitor's experience is, ultimately, to maximize and deepen those experiences. The authors, Radbourne, Glow and Johanson, identify four key intrinsic attributes of the audience experience: knowledge, risk, authenticity, and collective engagement. Identifying such attributes of the audience experience, and providing a means of measurement, is critical in thinking about how the audience is (or could be) at the core of the mission of arts organizations.

Radbourne, Glow and Johanson show that the audience's experience of collective engagement in the arts can be derived from the intimacy of the venue. The issue of the place or setting for the audience experience is further explored in the following three chapters. The various research projects outlined by Barker (Chapter 2), Glow (Chapter 3) and Brown (Chapter 4) are all interested in how settings influence the arts experience for audiences. For Barker the 'setting' is the digital environment in which the relatively new concept of the digital streaming of live performing arts into cinemas is becoming an established practice. Barker focuses on the 'liveness' of this experience and rejects the assertions that audiences of digital streaming cannot engage with performers or interact with other audience members to derive the intensified experience of participation. Barker's access to data from the New York Metropolitan Opera and NESTA's attendees at the National Theatre provides a significant sample articulating their 'engagement' and responses to the 'live' event.

For Glow (Chapter 3) the notion of setting refers to the community or neighbourhood from which the audience is drawn. In particular, she looks at a project at the Theatre Royal Stratford East which is dedicated to building audience engagement through the development of co-curatorial relationships with community members. Through a volunteer programme, this arts organization is listening to the voices and stories of those in the community that are not often heard, and in so doing is building a sense of empowerment and ownership of the theatre by the local community. Such a participative approach to arts programming, she argues, represents a radical shift in traditional notions of cultural authority.

For Brown (Chapter 4) the setting for the arts refers to the physical environment within which audiences engage with the arts. He examines the role that settings play in determining the experience of a performance and argues that the arts sector has not yet developed sufficiently critical thinking about the changing nature of arts venues and settings, or a nuanced understanding of how setting influences the audience's arts experience. Different settings can enhance or detract from participation in contemporary arts experiences. In particular, Brown identifies that younger audiences attach great importance to settings and format.

This exploration of meaning-making within certain specific arts contexts is followed by a group of chapters that explore different aspects of the audience experience in terms of the quality and depth of that experience. Lois Foreman-Wernet and Brenda Dervin (Chapter 5) use Dervin's Sense-Making Methodology to inform interviews that elicit deep self-reflection on the part of audience members. The categories they identify as central to the audience experience are: truth/beauty, captivation, self-expression, self-awareness, cognitive/intellectual growth, community/connection, well-being and social judgement. In a case study of audience members at a classical music concert, Foreman-Wernet and Dervin identify lack of prior knowledge of classical music and a sense of peer pressure and elitist social judgement as being the main obstacles to attending and getting personal benefit from a concert.

Stephanie Pitts (Chapter 6) is also interested in audiences for live music performance. She looks at a particular audience group – jazz and classical listeners – to investigate the reciprocal relationships between playing and listening. Conventionally seen as a delivery process from expert performer to receptive listener, the interaction of playing and listening is misunderstood when it does not acknowledge the effects that prior experience of instrumental playing have on a listener's perspective. Pitts' study confirms her earlier research establishing that experiential knowledge of performance heightens a listener's awareness of the process of performing. Using a range of data-gathering tools – including questionnaires, interviews and diaries – Pitts explores the attitudes of audiences to specific events, performers and genres in order to understand the experience of live music for a range of listeners. Pitts' study finds that audience members with some experience as players have an enhanced concert experience. Further, their previous playing experience is a factor in audiences' listening choices. Such research into the value of live listening, Pitts argues, invites a consideration of the role live music listening plays in inspiring a lifetime of musical engagement.

Matthew Reason (Chapter 7) is concerned with the quality of the audience experience, with a particular focus on younger audiences. Reason explores a specific question: how is it that a highly successful dance performance for young people, performed over five hundred times around the world and acclaimed by critics, was considered to be poor quality by a group of Scottish schoolchildren? Reason investigates the cause of this discrepancy, suggesting that the children's indifference to the performance arose from their belief that the vernacular style of dance was not the result of professional competence and from the absence of spoken dialogue between the performers. Reason suggests that the children were not supported to engage with the performance. In the second half of the chapter, he identifies the kind of reflective dialogue that is facilitated by his own research with young audiences after the performance, and as pursued by Scottish organization Imaginate, as holding the key to extending children's experience of a performance beyond the performance itself and enhancing their engagement.

In the final section of the book, a selection of authors discusses new methods for gathering data on the audience experience. Methodological innovation is important in the field as it helps to produce a nuanced reading of how audiences make meaning and are engaged by the arts. These chapters make a valuable contribution to our understanding of how audience data is collected, and how that method can influence audience engagement and thereby its capacity to take artistic risks with the company.

Lisa Baxter, Daragh O'Reilly and Elizabeth Carnegie (Chapter 8) critique the limitations of arts marketing literature with its traditional focus on mapping arts consumption (this issue is further explored and reinforced by Radbourne's research in Chapter 10). The authors suggest that research participants can also co-create research. Baxter, O'Reilly and Carnegie engineer a new methodology that repositions the research participants as active partners in the research process, rather than just data providers.

Kim Vincs (Chapter 9) argues that audience engagement is vital to dance companies if they are creating new work with the expectation of attracting audiences. Vincs bases her analysis on a series of experiments in which she asked audience members to record their continuous levels of engagement with the dance works they were watching using hand-held palm pilot devices. The aim of her research is to discover how consistent (or diverse) audiences' responses are, and whether specific choreographic structures can be shown to enhance the audiences' engagement. In particular, Vincs identifies the importance of what she terms 'gem moments': moments associated with shifts in expectation generated by dynamic shifts in the movement. Vincs finds that while there is considerable variation between observers, there is also significant agreement within the responses, which indicates that there are common elements of choreographic phrasing in the dances that influence engagement. For Vincs, innovation is the driver of contemporary dance creation and marketing, and her research suggests firstly that audience engagement with innovation can be mapped and secondly that this mapping demonstrates high levels of agreement in responding to particular choreographic phrasing. Such research has the potential to inform dance aesthetics and the development of new dance works which attract and engage audiences.

Following Baxter, O'Reilly and Carnegie, Jennifer Radbourne (Chapter 10) addresses the importance of co-creation in the arts experience. Radbourne argues that arts marketing theory needs to acknowledge and address a new emphasis on the consumer's desire for self-actualisation in their experience of the arts. Audience members seek a co-creative role when they attend the arts, and a form of creative fulfilment that is not yet sufficiently addressed or understood in arts marketing practice or literature.

To conclude, Katya Johanson (Chapter 11) argues that innovative research methodologies are needed to identify and encapsulate the complexity of audience experiences. She reviews a number of projects that have sought to introduce new ways of gathering data, including several earlier studies by authors represented in this book. In Johanson's view, new audience research needs to capture the apparently inexpressible qualities, depth and intensity of these experiences.

In summary, this book represents a shift in the way we research audiences. Where audience research has tended to be restricted to the collection of data on visitor satisfaction and attendance rates, the chapters in this book introduce research findings and new methods for data collection that investigate the nature of audience members' experience in a performance, and how to identify, record and examine these experiences. Such insights will prompt new conversations between audience researchers and performing arts practitioners.

Elaine Acworth, writing in a performing arts blog, sums up these themes:

I think, in a good piece of work, an audience can expand the meaning that they read there. I think there's a space made in the work – in that place mid-way between the actors and participants sitting in the dark – where the possibility of layered meanings exists – the resonances of the individual audience member's life making themselves heard in and around the performance.

(Acworth 2009)

References

Acworth, E. (2009), 'What Do Audiences Want?', www.ourbrisbane.com/blogs/performing-arts/2009-02-17-what-do-audiences-want. (accessed 19 March 2009).

Australian Art Orchestra Focus Group (2011), 18 July, Melbourne Australia.

Brown, A.S. & Novak, J.L. (2007), *Assessing the Intrinsic Impacts of a Live Performance*, WolfBrown. http://www.wolfbrown.com/mups_downloads/Impact_Study_Final_Version_full.pdf. (accessed 4 September 2012).

Foreman-Wernet, L. (2010), 'Marketing the Arts Audience: Questioning Our Aim(s)', in L. Foreman-Wernet & B. Dervin (eds) *Audiences and the Arts: Communication Perspectives*, Cresskill, NJ: Hampton Press Inc.

KAGE Focus Group (2011), 10 April, Castlemaine, Victoria Australia.

Kahneman, D. (2010), 'The Riddle of Experience vs. Memory', TED Talks, http://www.ted.com/talks/daniel_kahneman_the_riddle_of_experience_vs_memory.html. (accessed 20 April 2010).

Pitts, S.E. (2005), *Valuing Musical Participation*, Aldershot: Ashgate.

Radbourne, J., Johanson, K. Glow, H. & White, T. (2009), 'The Audience Experience: Measuring Quality in the Performing Arts', *International Journal of Arts Management*, 11: 3, pp. 16–29.

Victorian Opera Focus Group (2011), 25 May, Melbourne Australia.

Chapter 1

Knowing and Measuring the Audience Experience

Jennifer Radbourne, Hilary Glow and Katya Johanson

The Toronto-based company Mammalian Diving Reflex produces performances in collaboration with children and young people. One of the company's most successful and frequently performed works is *Haircuts by Children*. The production involves a group of local children aged between 10 and 12 who are trained in basic hairdressing skills by a professional stylist. Working in a rented hair salon, the participants offer free haircuts to members of the public. The idea that children should be allowed to cut the hair of adults is part of the vision of the company to consider children and young people as creative participants; people whose aesthetic choices can and should be trusted. The artistic director Darryl O'Donnell notes that he had expected the outcome to be anarchic 'with hair flying all over the place but, in reality, with kids taking the responsibility so seriously, the mood in the salon becomes almost sombre. The kids focus total attention on the task at hand' (O'Donnell 2007). Another unanticipated outcome of the event is that an intimacy develops between the young haircutters and their adult clients, with small quiet conversations taking place between them. 'It is the idea of a stranger handing over trust to a child' (O'Donnell 2007).

Haircuts by Children is a performance work that is interested in engagement. The conventionally understood line between performer and audience is blurred, and in this performance 'space' a new kind of engaged interaction occurs. Here, all participants simultaneously both produce and respond to an aesthetic experience that is taking place all around them. It is a profound performance 'happening'; it is intense, intimate, risky, absorbing, authentic (the haircuts are actually happening), and an experience that is shared by all who are present. So thorough is audience engagement in *Haircuts by Children* that the audience and the art offering have become one.

While *Haircuts by Children* might be seen as unconventional, it encapsulates some of the new thinking around audience engagement. It might be seen to be an extreme example, more in line with Ben Cameron's argument that 'many in today's arts reformation question the necessity of professional artists in a creative artistic experience' (quoted in Wallace Foundation 2012: 3). Mammalian Diving Reflex have made a connection between performance and audience enfranchisement and while not all performing arts organizations are dedicated to the same goal, the performing arts sector is changing. Performing arts audiences are seeking more engaged forms of participation and arts organizations are developing ways to broaden, deepen and diversify their audiences (Wallace Foundation 2012).

Audience engagement and artistic vibrancy

Although slow to become the subject of academic study, audience engagement is a leading research concern of contemporary arts industry and funding bodies such as the Australia Council (2010, 2011a, 2011b), the Arts Council of England (2010/2011), the Urban Institute (Walker & Sherwood 2003), the Wallace Foundation (2012), the New Economic Foundation (2010) and the RAND Corporation (McCarthy et al. 2004). The research reports commissioned or produced by these organizations are largely motivated by two complementary contentions: first, that building audiences is the key to the survival and well-being of the arts sector; and second, that many contemporary audiences want to be more thoroughly engaged in an arts experience than is conventionally supposed. The aim of these reports is to identify the factors that contribute to audience engagement and/or to identify strategies to build it by, in the words of Wallace Foundation (2012), 'broadening, deepening and diversifying' the audience experience. For these organizations, and the many arts organizations that use their findings, audience engagement is a fundamental concern.

There is a growing argument that audience engagement actually contributes to or is an important element of the institution's innovation and, in the Australia Council's words 'artistic vibrancy'. In their 2010 National Endowment for Science, Technology and the Arts (NESTA) report, Hasan Bakhshi and David Throsby argue that 'audience reach' is one of the four core elements of artistic innovation. According to Bakhshi and Throsby, innovation in 'audience reach' results from the strategies that institutions and companies use to broaden their audience, deepen their audience and diversify their audience (2010: 4).

Bakhshi and Throsby found that innovation in the delivery of exhibitions and productions allowed both the Tate Gallery and the UK National Theatre to attract broader and more diverse audiences. They focused particularly on the use of online technology in delivery. For example, they found that in the case of the Tate, online exhibitions attracted a greater proportion of ethnically diverse visitors, of younger visitors and of lower income visitors than do exhibitions in the Gallery's physical space. The Tate and the National Theatre could argue that increasing their audience reach is an indication of their innovation, even if the total number of visitors is not increased.

In terms of audience 'deepening', Bakhshi and Throsby found that innovative delivery to visitors and audiences often increased the depth of their experience, and certainly did not detract from the depth of experience that was cultivated through conventional delivery. Here, their focus was very much on online exhibitions (in the case of the Tate) or synchronous televised performances (in the case of the National Theatre).

In contrast, organizational efforts to simply focus on the extent of demand or financial return may discourage innovation, as the UK's New Economic Foundation (NEF) report found:

> The kinds of measurement that are currently prevalent in the theatre sector do not seem to encourage work that is concordant with the actual artistic motivations of theatre

professionals. For instance, in terms of both the number and the diversity of people who attend performances, one theatre company noted that its audience development targets 'will be lower for new work ... and far fewer people will see it. But it is this work that most often touches and resonates with individuals, affecting their lives and sometimes their futures, in a profound way'.

(ITC, Society of London Theatre, TMA 2010: 9)

Similarly, Bakhshi and Throsby found that at the National Theatre, there was a 'trade-off between increased audience and programming new work. As with the theatre, popular art shows attract large crowds, whereas more experimental work gets smaller attendances. Predictions from our econometric demand equations ... show that, other things equal, expected aggregate attendance and revenue at a contemporary show are likely to be up to 20 per cent lower than for a modern show' (Bakhshi & Throsby 2010: 41).

It is becoming increasingly clear within the arts sector that measuring ticket buying or attendance is not sufficient to provide knowledge of audience engagement (Walmsley 2011; Radbourne, Johanson, Glow & White 2009). For several years there was a trend for arts policy and funding to measure and ascribe to the arts 'instrumental' qualities, such as reducing crime, increasing tourism or increasing literacy rates. In response, there is now a movement to identify and measure the 'intrinsic qualities' of the arts, whether these be artistic excellence, innovation or vibrancy. In the United States, for example, the Wallace Foundation's RAND report catalogues the benefits of arts experiences and argues that future assessment of these benefits should focus on intrinsic, artistic qualities rather than apparent economic or social benefits (McCarthy et al. 2004). In the UK, the cultural policy critic John Holden, amongst others, has argued that the emphasis on the instrumental benefits of the arts has been detrimental to cultural production. Such research argues that arts organizations are inclined to place too much emphasis either on financial or demand-based indicators of success, such as ticket sales and attendance figures. Meanwhile, there has been too little emphasis on what Turbide and Laurin call 'true mission fulfilment' (2009: 61).

How is audience engagement measured?

As a result of such critiques, the systems by which the success of artists and organizations is measured needs to be reconsidered. Rather than measuring demand metrics in order to demonstrate the success or failure of arts productions, we should look at how audiences are engaged with the performance. Alan Brown and Jennifer Novak, whose research is described in more detail below, describe the centrality of this engagement in relation to the performing arts:

The true impact ... is what happens to individual audience members when the lights go down and the artist takes the stage – and the cumulative benefits to individuals, families and communities of having those experiences available night after night, year after year.

(Brown & Novak 2007: 5)

As the cultural or aesthetic experience is the chief focus of the arts organization or institution, it is this experience that should be the chief focus of an assessment of such organizations' success.

These arguments in support of a case for measuring the intrinsic qualities associated with the arts experience have, not surprisingly, led to a discussion of how to go about researching intrinsic qualities of the audience experience. In establishing our own framework for measuring audience engagement, we reviewed a number of recent alternative measures, including *Capturing the audience experience* (UK NEF report); Alan Brown and Jennifer Novak's 2007 US study, *Assessing the intrinsic impact of a live performance*; and Nusser Raajpoot, Khoon Koh and Anita Jackson's (2010) research which established a scale to measure service quality in museums.

While the first study focuses on gallery and theatre audiences, the second focuses on the performing arts and the third focuses on museums, the three studies are discussed in this chapter on the performing arts because they have much in common in terms of identifying the qualities of audience experience. In recognition of the fact that 'one person's experience may be quite different from another's' they all set out to measure the *dimensions* or attributes of the audience/visitor experience rather than the details (NEF 2010: 11). All use audience interviews or focus groups to establish these attributes, which form the basis of a survey used to measure the experience of individual company productions or museum exhibitions. Furthermore, the Raajpoot, Koh and Jackson study is included here because there is still relatively little literature on audience engagement in the performing arts (Walmsley 2011).

Raajpoot, Koh and Jackson developed a scale to measure the quality of service at museums, with the aim of assisting museums to 'deliver high-quality experiences that result in higher levels of loyalty and profitability' (2010: 54). Their study of museum visitors gave rise to ten domains of museum evaluation by audiences, including *Pleasure*, which has been 'defined as the joy one feels when viewing beautiful or aesthetically pleasing objects that add value to the museum experience'; *Relaxation* or the relief of stress as visitors to the museum 'get away from the usual demands of life'; *Learning*, including challenge or the satisfaction of curiosity and a sense of discovery; *Entertainment* or the enjoyment of a social outing; *Solitude*, as many visitors seek to get away from others and to 'internalize and meditate on the visit'; *Self-actualization* or a way for individuals to seek solace and secure images of the self; *Social recognition*, as visitors sense that others will think more highly of them and that they will impress others by demonstrating their intelligence or knowledge; *Courtesy*, defined as politeness, willingness or generosity in providing something, as experienced from museum employees; *Spatial design* of the museum building and exhibitions; and *Aesthetics*, or the appreciation of beauty and good taste (Raajppot, Koh & Jackson 2010: 58–59).

Table 1.1: The three reports find several common attributes to classify the audience experience

Raajpoot, Koh & Jackson	NEF	Brown & Novak
Pleasure	Engagement and concentration	Captivation
Relaxation		
Learning	Learning and challenge	Intellectual stimulation
Entertainment	Shared experience and atmosphere	Social bonding
Social recognition		
Self-actualization	Personal resonance and emotional connection	Spiritual value
Solitude		
Courtesy		
Spatial design		
Aesthetics		Aesthetic growth
	Energy and tension	

The aim of measuring the audience or visitor's experience of these attributes is, ultimately, to maximize them: to 'deepen' their experience of the performance or exhibition. Brown and Novak argue that the audience member's ability to experience these attributes depends on the existence of three 'readiness constructs', which can be measured prior to the performance. Readiness constructs consist of 'context', or how much experience and knowledge the individual has about the performance and the performers; 'relevance' – an individual's level of comfort with the performance experience, such as whether they are in a familiar social or cultural setting; and 'anticipation', or the individual's psychological state prior to the performance, situated along a continuum from low to high expectations.

Researchers are already identifying and assessing audience engagement to articulate and demonstrate the value of arts productions and exhibitions and to assess their success in meeting artistic aims. When identifying the innovation of the Tate Gallery in 'deepening' its visitors' experience, for example, Bakhshi and Throsby solicited agreement against statements such as 'I was totally absorbed', 'I was transported', 'I had an emotional response', 'It did not engage intellectually', 'Wanted to talk afterwards', 'Not seeing it with other people made it less enjoyable' and 'Increased my understanding of contemporary art'.

The audience experience index

The authors have been researching measures of audience engagement against attributes of the audience experience. We have conducted focus groups and audience surveys of a group of Australian small-medium performing arts organizations. For each organization, researchers conducted focus groups with both regular attenders (subscribers) and those who had not previously attended. Each focus group was posed questions which invited participants to reflect on the experience of a performance they had just seen. We found there were consistent reflections across the groups and, through cross-analysis, four key attributes of the audience experience emerged: knowledge, risk, authenticity, and collective engagement.

The term *knowledge* is used here to describe how audiences seek information as part of their engagement; they seek understanding, intellectual stimulation, and cognitive growth. One of the respondents commented: 'That's why you go – so that you can actually get something [from it] that will hopefully make you think about your life in general.' Statements like this revealed an understanding of the role of knowledge or learning as part of the audience experience as a means of prompting further thought and discussion. On the other hand, a perceived lack of knowledge was seen to be a disadvantage or an alienating factor for some audience members: 'I find live performance quite difficult. ... [W]hen people started laughing ... it's like, are they in the know? ... Did they know the people, did they know stuff about the play? I mean, I don't know anything about it ... I didn't know [he] wrote plays'. Comments of this ilk expressed a sense of discomfort about not being sufficiently 'in the know' to value what was seen. Such responses suggest that some audiences feel there is hidden knowledge within the experience of viewing live performing arts which speaks to a cognoscenti but can challenge those not 'in the know'.

The term *risk* is used here to describe the various forms of risk that performing arts audiences experience: this can be economic risk (Have I wasted my money?), psychological risk (Will I feel okay about the experience?), or social risk (Will I fit in?). *Risk* can be seen as the gap between expectation and perception; in Brown and Novak's terms, it tells us about the audience's state of 'readiness'. A respondent commented that

> [In stand-up comedy and live music] there's a lot of interaction and ... the performer is trying to get ... audience participation and feedback. But in theatre I think it's more like art on the wall in that it's about how the audience perceive it without having much interaction ... you can't get any information from the performer as to whether he wants you to laugh or be silent so I find that quite difficult which may well be one of the main reasons why I don't go and see a lot of live theatre.

This response speaks to the issue of risk and readiness as it identifies the importance (for some) to have a sense of what is expected of them as audience members. Indeed, in this case, a lack of clarity about expectations, particularly when there was no encouragement from the performers, led to a sense of disappointment with the live-performance experience. On the other hand, some audience members revealed a high capacity or appetite for risk: 'This isn't risky theatre because it lives up to my expectation of being in-your-face. Risky theatre is subscribing to the mainstream theatre companies and taking the risk that you'll be bored witless.' This comment indicates how audience members can self-identify with a company's selection of productions; they want to take emotional risks, be challenged and expect to take a personal risk in attending.

We use the descriptor *authenticity* to capture the way audiences seek truth and believability, artistic authenticity and emotional engagement in their valuing of the live performing arts. An audience member commented: 'Many of the [play] topics are ones which, after you have watched them, you do consider and reflect on in your own life.' Audiences seek to learn more about themselves and society from attendance, and this response by an audience member underlines the feeling that the theatre being produced had an authenticity for them as they related the play's themes to their own lives. Another member commented: 'I am always quite excited about coming because they are usually new plays, quite often they are premieres … something I have not seen before and something I am going to have to think about. I really like the idea that it is a small ensemble … and I feel I get to know a lot of the actors and I really enjoy that.' This comment suggests there is a correlation between 'quality' and 'authenticity'; high 'quality' performance practice is associated with the audience's quest for 'authentic' experiences.

Finally, we use the term *collective engagement* as a way of describing the audience's sense that there are communal meanings; that they value the relationship to performers, the shared enjoyment with other audience members, and the sense of social inclusion that can accompany the experience of attending the live performing arts. One member commented: '[Y]ou have a connection individually about how it is affecting you, and then sometimes you may be swept up with others'. Audience responses like this one suggest the importance of audience-to-audience interaction; that the co-presence of others in the venue and, sometimes, the ability to discuss the performance afterwards can be significant factors in heightening the audience experience.

These four indicators comprise an index of the audience experience and we were compelled to design a measurement tool that could be used by arts companies to determine how successful they are in providing the appropriate experience for their audiences. Such a tool may replace traditional data collection which measures satisfaction and cross-reference attendance patterns with demographics. The Arts Audience Experience Index (AAEI) is conceived as a tool to access audience data on the intrinsic benefits of their experience of the performance. Most current audience data is collected at the point of purchase or in qualitative focus groups or quantitative surface level satisfaction surveys. This is the first tool developed to measure the engagement of audience members with the performance and the performers. The Index identifies the value of each of the indicators to the audience at that performance.

An interval scale of 1–5 is used for each indicator to facilitate easy transfer of the median results of survey questions using a Likert Scale of 1–5 (where 1 is low and 5 is high). A simple survey distributed to audience members includes a bank of eight statements of importance, and eight statements of agreement. These statements are developed around the attributes of each indicator, customized for the particular arts organization. Two statements in each bank relate to the Experience Indicators. The median result is used for each statement. The statement results are summated and the mean used to determine the Experience Indicator.

Table 1.2: The Arts Audience Experience Index

	Audience experience quality indicators	Attributes of each indicator	Metric rating
(a)	Knowledge transfer or learning	Extent to which there is contextual programming, visual enhancements, programme information, pre-show or conductor talks or meet the director after-the-show talks. These strategies function to facilitate new understandings, linking experience to self-knowledge and self-development in audience members.	1–5
(b)	Risk management	Commitment to managing risk, through programme knowledge, previews, comfort and accessibility, personalized communication, quality guarantee expectation, value for money.	1–5
(c)	Authenticity	Capacity to achieve believability, meaning and representation, sincerity, performance matches promotional description, performers engaged in own performances, performers' relationship with audience.	1–5
(d)	Collective engagement	Ensuring expectations of social contact and inclusion are met, including shared experience, social constructs and meaning, common values, live experience, interaction or understanding between performers and audience, clues to behaviour, discussion after the performance.	1–5

The Index is based on the sum of (a) + (b) + (c) + (d). Each indicator is rated from 1–5 and the total provides the score for the arts organization:

- 4–7 = minimal quality audience experience;
- 8–11 = moderate quality audience experience;
- 12–16 = moderately high quality audience experience;
- 17–20 = high quality audience experience.

Individual indicators (or the total score out of 20) can be used in analysing the organization's achievements in building their audience experience.

The Index was applied to two performing arts organizations in Victoria, Australia: one a small contemporary theatre company and the other a regional performing arts centre. The data provided explicit feedback on the quality indicators of the AAEI, that is the audiences' need for, and use of, information to understand the performance; their pre-disposition to risk and willingness to take artistic risks in partnership with the company; their search for believability and quality; and finally, their behavioural responses in relating to performers and other audience members.

A focus group was used with the theatre company audience members and a survey with the arts centre audience members. Both included common questions which prompted the respondents to reflect on the nature of their experience as audience members and to consider a variety of elements which enhanced or detracted from that experience. Participants were asked to reflect on their responses to the performance, such as when they felt most engaged in the performance, what prompted this engagement, what emotions were elicited and how they expressed this emotion.

Focus group participants were volunteers recruited by the company from their subscriber list. In terms of knowledge, this audience did not seek prior knowledge on the show, because they already had an understanding of the ensemble, the actors, types of productions and had already made the decision to subscribe or attend based on that knowledge and expectation. This audience attends because they want to be emotionally and intellectually challenged. They want to learn more about themselves and society from attendance. They certainly want the learning provided by these productions but they do not need information to prepare them. They have that intrinsically.

Respondents stated that they were happy to attend with friends or alone. They did not need to come with others because their collective engagement is derived from the intimacy of the venue and the fact that they expect those who attend are similar to themselves and will all experience the performance as one. They believe that the audience is sharing the same emotional and intellectual experience whether they attended solo or with a group.

Respondents clearly stated that they seek risk and this is why they attend performances by this company. They self-identify with the company's selection of productions. They want to take emotional risks. They want to be challenged. They expect to have to take a personal risk in attending a performance. They also expect quality. Their search for authenticity is about quality. They know that the acting will be memorable and the direction and design will deliver on their expectations. Authenticity is also associated with the intimacy of the venue. They would not attend if the venue was larger or if the quality diminished. The findings indicated a high rating for capacity to take risks and need for authenticity, and a low rating for need for pre-show knowledge and purposeful collective engagement. The implications of this are that if the company wishes to grow its audiences then they may have to develop a second company or programme that tours or performs for a different (festival, arts centre) audience while maintaining the subscription audience and their intrinsic benefits derived at the current venue.

The second use of the Index was for a regional arts centre which programmes its subscription season around the two drivers of product availability and audience preference. The artistic policy, as stated by the general manager, was such that one show in the season presented a 'risk' to audiences, as a means to develop, aesthetically, the audiences in that region. A face-to-face survey questionnaire was used with 25 audience members, most of whom were members of the arts centre Theatre Club. The survey contained a set of context-setting questions before the questions testing the Experience Indicators. The responses to the early questions showed an expectation of entertainment, fast-moving dialogue, a well-written play with performances of a high quality.

The banks of statements on the attributes of the indicators revealed that the most important aspect of attendance or participation in a performance for these audience members is the quality of the performers and programme notes. It is not important that they have previous knowledge of this work or that it is part of a festival, but they do want to talk about the performance with others after the show. The audience showed the highest value for authenticity, that is, believable and sincere performances and engagement with the performers. Their second highest value or intrinsic benefit was collective engagement; that is, sharing their experience with other audience members during or after the show. They showed a lower value for knowledge and risk, revealing an expectation that the company or arts centre would provide the information needed to understand the performance and that the production would be what they preferred and at an acceptable cost, neither requiring personal research nor personal risk. This data was analysed and the index calculated and reported to the company.

Our research is in agreement with the Australia Council's (2010) *More than Bums on Seats* report when it argues that 'if the link between the arts and the wide ranging benefits they deliver could be more strongly established it would add even greater value to the arts'. We know that the arts compete with other mediated cultural engagement but that the social needs for a connected society and the re-assertion of the spiritual value of the arts and the individual's quest for authenticity contribute to the aesthetic development of the art form at the highest level. Satisfaction and service data ignore these values. There is a clear need to adopt the means to measure the audience experience because measurement is followed by action, purpose, innovation, change and growth. Acknowledgement and measurement explicitly links programming to a business development model where the audience is at the core of the company's mission.

This book addresses the need for research into key aspects of the felt responses of arts audiences while acknowledging the difficulties (both methodological and theoretical) inherent in the process. Despite the great investment of the last 20 years in developing strategic marketing knowhow, we do not know enough about – and do not know how to describe – the benefits that audiences derive from arts experiences. As Brown and Novak point out: 'Many who work in the arts, including those of us who do so because of our belief in the transformative power of art, lack a vernacular for communicating its impacts' (Brown & Novak 2007: 5). The authors in this collection demonstrate that if we are able to move beyond thinking of audience research in terms of collecting data on visitor satisfaction, we can start to conceive of how arts attendance relates to the intrinsic benefits of cultural engagement. In so doing we can develop a deep and detailed understanding of how the arts affect the lives of those who engage with them.

References

Australia Council for the Arts (2010), *More than Bums on Seats: Australian Participation in the Arts* Sydney: Australia Council for the Arts.
——— (2011a), *Connecting://Arts Audiences Online*, Sydney: Australia Council for the Arts, June.

——— (2011b), *Artistic Vibrancy Audience Impact Survey*, Sydney: Australia Council for the Arts, May.

Bakhshi, H. & Throsby, D. (2010), *Culture of Innovation: an Economic Analysis of Innovation in Arts and Cultural Organizations*, NESTA Research Report, June.

Brown, A.S. and Novak, J.L. (2007), *Assessing the Intrinsic Impacts of a Live Performance*, WolfBrown, http://www.wolfbrown.com/mups_downloads/Impact_Study_Final_Version_full.pdf. (accessed 10 June 2011).

Holden, J. (2004), *Capturing Cultural Value: How Culture Has Become a Tool of Government Policy*, London: Demos.

Kennedy, D. (2010), *The Spectator and the Spectacle: Audiences in Modernity and Postmodernity*, Cambridge: Cambridge University Press.

McCarthy, Kevin F., Ondaatje, E.H., Zakaras, L. & Brooks, A. (2004), *Gifts of the Muse: Reframing the Debate about the Benefits of the Arts*, RAND Corporation, February, http://www.wallacefoundation.org/KnowledgeCenter/KnowledgeTopics/CurrentAreasofFocus/ArtsParticipation/Pages/gifts-of-the-muse.aspx. (accessed 15 November 2011).

M.R. (2006), 'A-F', *Performance Research*, 11: 3, pp. 1–60.

New Economic Foundation (2010), *Capturing the Audience Experience: A Handbook for the Theatre*, ITC, SOLT, TMA.

O'Donnell, D. (2007), 'Greasing the Glue and Gluing the Grease: Beautiful Civic Engagement with Kids, by Kids, for Kids', *New Quarterly*, Issue 101 (Winter).

Pitts, S. (2005), 'What Makes an Audience? Investigating the Roles and Experiences of Listeners at a Chamber Music Festival', *Music & Letters*, 86: 2, pp. 257–269.

Raajpoot, N., Koh, K. & Jackson, A. (2010), 'Developing a Scale to Measure Service Quality', *International Journal of Arts Management*, 12: 3, pp. 54–69.

Radbourne, J., Johanson, K., Glow, H. & White, T. (2009), 'Audience Experience: Measuring Quality in the Performing Arts', *International Journal of Arts Management*, 11: 3 (Spring), pp. 16–29.

Turbide, J. & Laurin, C. (2009), 'Performance Measurement in the Arts Sector: The Case of the Performing Arts', *International Journal of Arts Management*, 11: 2, pp. 56–70.

Walmsley, B. (2011), 'Why People Go to the Theatre: A Qualitative Study of Audience Motivation', *Journal of Customer Behaviour*, 10: 4, pp. 335–351.

Wallace Foundation (2003), *Building Arts Organizations that Build Audiences*, New York: Wallace Foundation.

Walker, C. & Sherwood, K. (2003), *Arts Participation: Steps to Stronger Cultural and Community Life*, Washington DC: Urban Institute.

Zamir, T. (2010), 'Watching Actors', *Theatre Journal*, 62: 2 (May), pp. 227–243.

Chapter 2

'Live at a Cinema Near You': How Audiences Respond to Digital Streaming of the Arts

Martin Barker

'Live Screenings to the Cinema': this headline in the programme for the Aberystwyth Arts Centre is at one level completely ordinary, and certainly comprehensible to its readers. At another level it might be read as profoundly challenging, even paradoxical. Either way, it signals very clearly the delivery to one small town of a recent phenomenon that is already having some quite far-reaching effects on cinemas and is certain to have many more. In this chapter, I will explore some of the consequences and implications of this phenomenon, which usually goes by the very bland name of 'Alternative Content'.

What is Alternative Content? It is the industry name for the digital transmission to cinemas of performances of opera, theatre, ballet and music – currently the prime exemplars. These performances are filmed at source in front of a regular audience, who both watch it for themselves (in what has to be uninterrupted and unaffected ways) and also provide an ambience of audience responses for those watching at a distance. They are then beamed simultaneously to audiences gathered in a wide range of places, often internationally. Although there are clear historical precedents for this phenomenon, dating at least to the 1930s, in its contemporary form it has a precise starting point, when the New York Metropolitan Opera 'broadcast' some of its 2006 season to a range of digitally equipped cinemas around New York State. The success of this experiment caused ears to prick, and within two years it was being repeated, copied, expanded and refined. In 2009 it had grown sufficiently that one of the cinema industry's major resources, *Screen Digest*, published its first special report on it. It made this prediction:

> The market for alternative content has progressed from one that was almost entirely experimental and ad hoc, to one now in early market evolution. The steady growth of the digital screen base to over 12,000 globally has provided sufficient scale to experiment with new content offerings in cinemas, and to secure longer term and more original content arrangements. Globally, the market for alternative content was worth $45.7m in 2008, equivalent to 0.4 per cent of gross global box office revenues. This is expected at least to double to hit $104.6m in 2009. Moreover, the entire alternative content market will be worth $526.5m by 2014.
>
> (Jones & Hancock 2009)

Developments since 2009 make it likely that this prediction is an understatement. In just two years, many new players have entered the field: for instance, Sydney Opera House,

National Theatre Live and the Royal Opera House (London). International consortia are emerging, Arts Alliance Media is coordinating the distribution of events across many European countries and technical requirements have become codified. Sports events are being programmed for 2011–2012, with American basketball leading the way, and popular music events are planned (a special screening of the Grateful Dead movie, with a live Q&A, took place in April 2011). Experiments with 3D Live are underway,[1] but of course, such experimentation will inevitably produce its failures – one of the first of which may have been the UK Cheltenham Jazz Festival's decision to stream a performance by Jamie Cullum in early 2011. Ticket sales for the streamed performance were poor. But one failure does not dampen enthusiasm; rather it prompts reassessment. And one of the features of this new phenomenon is the amount of commercial research being conducted, to try to determine the nature of the audience, and their hopes and expectations. Most strikingly, in the UK the National Endowment for Science, Technology and the Arts (NESTA) conducted two rounds of very expensive research in 2009. NESTA was very much a creature of New Labour, interfacing government hopes to grow the UK economy through digital initiatives, with venture capital and university research links. Its research, provided confidentially to the major providers, showed the potential for audience growth and expansion from Alternative Content. Other providers have been conducting their own audience polls to try to predict success.

The implications of Alternative Content are far-reaching, impacting on the fields of political economy and business modelling, cultural politics and policy, cinema theory, and presentational aesthetics. For the purposes of this discussion, I will focus on audiences' experience of and participation in these events. Crucially, and perhaps most obviously, I want to explore the implications for our understanding of 'liveness'.

'Liveness'

In the opener to a UK *Guardian Weekend* 'special' in which a variety of commentators tried to characterize the 'noughties' decade (even before it had quite finished), playwright David Hare began a lament:

> In theatres up and down the country, it used to be that anyone, whatever their job, was pulled magnetically towards the stage. All through the day they would find themselves venturing down into the auditorium. They would casually try to catch a glimpse of the action, because that was where their job was rooted. Today, 10 years into the new century, theatre workers, like the rest of us, sit staring at computer screens all day, and sometimes all night. Hardly surprising, then, that this has been the Decade of Looking Away.
>
> (Hare 2009)

'Absence always trumps presence', he continued, generalizing his theatrical metaphor to an account of the 'Decade of Looking Away'. In this manner, issues of presence vs. distance, liveness vs. mediation were made symptomatic of a fearsome cultural loss tied by lines of influence to the war on terror, global recession, climate change, and a general climate of non-caring. Although an extreme case, the fact that this arguable claim (that theatres no longer have the 'pull of presence') could function indexically for a much wider set of liberal-intellectual concerns in the context of this chapter is of interest, in and of itself. Something big was at stake here. Theatre is felt to be the embattled preserve of a vital cultural value that signals *reality* as against such bad tendencies as 'distraction', 'insincerity' and 'hypocrisy' (all among Hare's terms). All these will more easily slip past our guard, where there is no 'presence'.

That a lot is at stake shows again in debates around the concept in contemporary cultural theorizing about 'liveness'. The concept is to be found, working quite differently, in a series of intellectual domains: notably theatre and performance studies, television studies, sports studies, comedy studies, new media/web studies and, to a small extent, cinema studies. Each of these has its own tradition of arguments, but each appears to operate in isolation from all the others.[2]

Although it is extremely risky to try to characterize all these debates in this constrained space, the issues are important enough to make the attempt necessary. Alternative Content crosses the borders between many art forms and traditions of thinking and any overall consideration of it has to take into account the burden of theory and assumptions each bears with it. In theatre and performance studies, then, 'liveness' comes with an imprimatur of importance – many practitioners insisting that it is key to the meaning and purpose of their work (see the debate between Phelan [1993] and Auslander [1999] for the main dimensions of this). But this insistence has been coloured by intense debates over a number of things: the politics of different performance styles and traditions, the penetration of technologies of production and reproduction in theatres, and the relations with other media such as television. Television studies, meanwhile, has had its own intense debate on the issues – but beginning, and insistently returning to, a completely opposite position: that 'liveness' may be a deceit practised by the medium on its audiences, a pretence to the absence of mediation and representation (see among others Ellis 1982; Feuer 1983; and Bourdon 2000).

Cinema studies, meanwhile, has only rarely directly encountered the concept, because of the wide assumption that films must be approached through the concepts of construction and representation. A minority interest in filming as 'ostension'– as an act of showing – which might have led to a direct debate about 'liveness' has remained just that, a minority interest (see Koven 2008: chapter 9). Therefore, it has mainly been when other fields have complained about films' impact on their preferred art form that 'liveness' has become an issue, most obviously when Shakespearian scholars have argued the lesser value of filmed drama (see Belsey 1998; and Keyishian 2008).

More recently, new media studies have taken up the issue of 'liveness' as a *challenge*, something to be achieved. So, research has been undertaken on how to make people feel co-present over the web – how in gaming to increase people's sense of proximity to avatars and other players, and generally how the 'virtual' of online worlds might be made to feel actual (see Palmer 2000).

The sports studies tradition has been very different. Based in sociology, work addressing the significance of 'liveness' has focused on the ways in which football fans, in particular, finding themselves excluded from matches (for financial, organizational and disciplinarian reasons), have recreated an approximation of the experience in other (e.g., pub) settings (see Weed 2007 and Crawford 2009). Another more minority interest within comedy studies, meanwhile, balances somewhat uneasily between these different approaches, with work focusing on the role of 'place' in stand-up comedy acts, centred on the common banter between performers and their audience over their locality – leading to assertions that recordings of live acts must lose some immediacy (see Scarpetta & Spagnolli 2009).

A critical examination of this array of differing traditions and debates brings into view some tricky dimensions. These are, with the exception of sports studies, heavily normative traditions. Writers are typically invested in trying to promote or preserve something they are committed to. The price of this is that some things are almost beyond debate. Most importantly, because of this, responses are regularly *imputed* to 'the audience', a fictive image commonly at work in cultural debates. This is therefore not about discovering what audiences may do, but about saying what they ought to, or need to do. But also, in many cases the concept of 'liveness' becomes gestural and nigh on impenetrable. It becomes an almost ineffable virtue, a 'something' to be valued or, in the case of television studies, distrusted. In fact, it seems to me that at least seven aspects of 'liveness' as grounds for cultural experience might usefully be distinguished:

1. Physical co-presence with performers and performance.
2. Simultaneity with the performance.
3. Direct engagement and absence of intervening (technological) mediation.
4. Sense of the 'local' within the experience.
5. Sense of interaction with performers.
6. Sense of interaction with others in the audience.
7. Intensified experiences/participation through sensing any of the above.

It is of course conceivable that these might all prove interdependent. But empirical audience research has to keep open the possibility that they might prove to function independently of, or even in conflict with, each other.

An emergent audience

So who attends these streamed performances, and what do we know about their responses and experiences? To answer this, I draw upon a number of surveys carried out by commercial organizations. NESTA compared responses from 1,316 cinemagoers with 1,216 theatregoers watching the National Theatre's *Phèdre*. The New York Met gathered 5,306 responses to a survey distributed to cinemas that were screening HD transmissions of their operas. Picturehouse conducted research among those on their email list, for the performances of *Ondine* (178 responses) and, more generally, for the Met Opera season (856 responses). I conducted one round of research in association with Picturehouse Cinemas (2009), using a quali-quantitative questionnaire that attracted 639 responses.[3] In broad terms, the five pieces of research appear to confirm each other. Each, however, asks some questions that the others do not. I offer a brief summary portrait, first.

This is, overall, a very appreciative audience. Levels of reported enthusiasm have been very high in all studies. In my own research, the numbers choosing 'Excellent' are striking, as Figure 2.1 indicates:

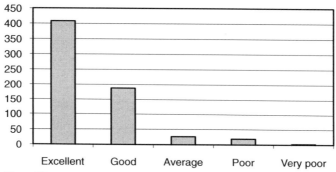

Figure 2.1

We will see shortly that this general enthusiasm masks concerns, and criticisms, and may be in part a 'novelty' response. The audience for Alternative Content is considerably older than normal cinema audiences, as indicated by this striking graph (Figure 2.2) from my research:

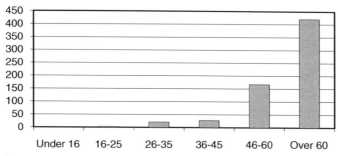

Figure 2.2

The Met's research, while broadly agreeing, did find a slightly higher proportion of younger audiences. This upwards age skew does have broad implications, not just in terms of a change in cinemas' reach, but also because of the different expectations that older audiences may have of venues (general facilities, noise management, intervals and the like). The pieces of research agree that more women than men attend these performances – with (in my survey) 60.7 per cent women to 39.3 per cent men. Women also reported higher levels of repeat attendance than men, particularly for the minority art form, ballet.

NESTA's research showed that cinema audiences for the National Theatre's productions had lower income levels than those attending the NT itself – although they were still predominantly middle-income. NESTA also measured audiences' expectations of the event, and then gauged their levels of involvement on a series of measures (e.g., absorption, emotional and cognitive engagements, being transported, creative stimulation, sensing others responding and excitement at its liveness). They found that while audiences at the cinema went in with lower expectations of the event, they reported consistently higher levels of emotional engagement than those at the theatre. Yet, most intriguingly, theatre and cinema attenders attached the same degree of attachment to the 'liveness' of the event. That has to mean that, for the cinema audiences, NT Live's streamed transmission counted sufficiently as 'live' for their purposes and pleasure. Unfortunately, NESTA's research design precluded further exploration of this. My research, and to some extent Picturehouse's, takes us further.

Picturehouse asked their respondents what difference it would make to their interest in attending future events if they knew it was recorded 24 hours previously. Interest in attending fell by a uniform 50 per cent for all kinds of events. It is clear that simultaneity is, at least for the moment, a significant factor. The New York Met asked their respondents if they would be interested in buying DVDs of the streamed events. The results were even more negative – and it is striking that to date there have been few cases of the filming of a streamed performance subsequently being made available on DVD. This again suggests that a differentiation is being made in audiences' minds between 'being there' and 'seeing it after the event'. What it also hints at, however, is a much more complicated and controversial thought: that for many in the audience, although it is evident the event is filmed and selections are made in that process, they do not regard or experience this as an act of mediation. Rather, they feel 'as if they are there', even perhaps in a privileged fashion.

My research also allowed me to explore the more complex relations between frequency of attending and evaluation of events. There is some evidence in my data of what I earlier referred to as a 'novelty factor'.

Although the base-numbers get quite small, the decline in enthusiasm in the second column looks to be an indication that people who attend for the first time may be impressed

Table 2.1: Relationship between frequency of attendance, and judgements of event

	First experience	Once previously	Twice previously	More than twice
Excellent	61.8%	51.9%	65.4%	66.3%
Good	28.5%	42.3%	21.1%	29.3%
Average	5.4%	5.8%	7.7%	3.4%
Poor	5.3%	0	5.8%	0.6%
Very poor	0	0	0	0.4%
Totals	56	52	52	474

by the novel experience; but people who attend a second time and have a point of comparison may begin to make critical comparisons. Those who keep returning, however, are becoming confident about these events, and are more likely to value the overall experience. What this suggests to me is that a proportion of the audience is learning and accepting particular 'manners of response and participation'. It is to these that I turn in the remainder of this chapter.

Audience conceptions of 'liveness'

The fact that many people gave their generalized approval to the Alternative Content events they attended half-concealed a range of criticisms, which they felt and spelt out in their discursive responses. In fact, some of those giving low ratings simply identified flaws in the technical provision: breakdowns in the streaming, uncontrolled sound levels, and the like. Others complained about the particular production they were seeing – usually disliking the singers in an opera. Some made a point of emphasizing that they were not criticizing the idea of streaming to cinemas – although within these, signs of a wider critique could sometimes be found, as here:

> This has nothing to do with the broadcast itself but rather the production. It was very clunky and overblown. No matter how long Renee Fleming went on about its marvels I found the production bordering on the grotesque. Unfortunately the vocal prowess of the leads is no longer enough to sustain an HD broadcast because of the close camerawork, thus it was impossible to engage with any of them or to believe in their romantic attachments. I think the Metropolitan's choice of this opera for an HD broadcast was a mistake.[4]

There are features in here to which I will return shortly: the knowingness of this critique (indeed the claim to a right to judge the Met's choices) and the combination of that with the idea of 'engagement'. To understand the force of this, we need to see the links with other features. These emerged from answers to two of my questions: 'In just a few words, can you tell us why you've given that rating?' and 'In what ways was watching this performance on a cinema screen like or unlike, and also better or worse, than actually being at the event itself?' Particularly among the answers to the second were some that offered an intriguing account of what 'liveness' means to respondents. A recurrent discursive feature was an admission/ withdrawal pairing, shown in the use of terms such as 'Obviously … but', as in these:

> Obviously nothing compares with being at a live performance, however, this is the next best thing.

> Obviously lacks the every night an event feel but the directed camera actually adds to emotional impact. I think this is a really valuable addition to the availability of arts.

Obviously not as good as actually being there but certainly the next best thing and the advantage being the backstage interviews.

Each of these answers takes as given that 'liveness' is valuable and therefore something is being lost in streamed performances, but then welcomes some aspect of the new situation. What interests me immediately is that which apparently does not need spelling out: the 'obvious' loss. The force of this unexplained element becomes more visible in the small number who were openly hostile to these events. For these, cinematic presentation was without question an act of mediation, and they did not like it. Here are three particularly strong illustrations of this:

Such a viewing cannot really compare with being in the actual theatre, as you are obliged to look at what the camera sees, not where you might wish to look. In addition, close-ups of singers/actors which cannot happen when viewing in the theatre can occasionally destroy the illusion that is built up by distance. The interval interviews and behind-the-scenes activities do add to the overall enjoyment.

Worse than being at the event because it was filmed like a television programme with close-ups and interviews. I wanted it to be exactly like being at the theatre seeing the whole stage all the time and being able to experience the spectacle (as well as not having it revealed to me that the young lovers were actually getting on a bit).

The camerawork has been very poor on occasions. In *Aïda* it drove me up the wall; there were so many occasions when we needed to see the set or the action straight on (grand march, etc.) but instead we got a diagonal shot. If you're used to seeing Egyptian imagery, seeing lots of diagonals just feels wrong. In *Tristan und Isolde* they used a split-screen effect which destroyed the point of the opera. You're supposed to drift trance-like into their world, not have it jazzed up! In the enthusiasm of giving us close-ups, sometimes we're not given enough control over our own eyes. For example, we don't have enough shots of the complete stage, often just at the beginning or end of the scene, so you lose the sense of the complete spectacle.

A critique is here being mounted in these responses that puts a quite specific gloss on what is involved in 'liveness'. This turns out to be a *doubled* process – at one and the same time having complete control (where and how to look, without direction) yet also giving up control (entering the presentation as an illusion). This is expressed particularly clearly in the third response, with that opposition between 'drifting trance-like into their world' and having 'control over our own eyes'. What bridges these, and makes them consistent, is the position of the viewer: s/he is sufficiently an expert to know how to look. And therefore it is apposite that critical voices of this kind tend to dislike being *told* the plot, being *shown* backstage and being *helped* to understand staging choices. For this reason I dubbed this an 'aficionado' orientation. Aficionados claim expertise for themselves, and require not to be guided or shown. 'Showing' amounts to interference, which is worse than simple mediation. Aficionados know how to build their own account and evaluation, because of their experience within their chosen art form. Only a small number in my response set adopt it completely (quite possibly because many of those who would adopt it outright simply avoid the screenings in the first place) but, as we will see, the degree of adoption of it relates strongly to acceptance or rejection of the purpose and workings of Alternative Content screenings. Liveness, therefore, for aficionados is much more than co-presence, simultaneity and the other dimensions I listed. It is most importantly a space and opportunity for their expert judgement, enabled by a highly managed mode of participation.

This doubling of responses is significant, not least for the nuances it adds to Pierre Bourdieu's very generalized account of people's relations with 'high culture'. In his *Distinction* (1984), Bourdieu argued that a high culture orientation was characterized by *knowing distance*, that is, a deliberately detached, even unenthusiastic way of participating in cultural events. I suspect that the combination of *insistent control* and *appropriate absorption* may be an art-centred equivalent of the 'strategic passivity' that we observed and identified in various researches into the audiences for mainstream films (see Barker & Brooks 1997; and Barker & Mathijs 2007).

Immersive responses

So, how should we characterize the alternative(s) to this? For many respondents, the experience was sufficiently powerful that they simply wanted to enthuse. So many answers never get beyond saying things like 'World class acting; world class singing', or 'Wonderful seeing a production that normally I could only read reviews of', or 'Exciting intimate and the best view in the house of the stage orchestra and backstage'. I have discussed elsewhere the disadvantages of pure enthusiasm for analytic purposes (Barker & Mathijs 2007: 152–3), and the curious advantage of expressions of disappointment because of their implied ideals (Barker & Brooks 1997: 225–39). But here, even in the shortest answers of this kind, there is a revealing feature: the emphasis on people's sense of *closeness* to the performances. This itself has several aspects: older audiences can find the sheer physical distance from the stage at a big venue challenging. Close-ups can overcome the problem, hence these kinds of responses:

It was good to see the faces of the singers and to be in comfortable seats.

I loved seeing the opera on screen. Close-up of the singers really helped, great to see them up close, especially the emotion in their faces. Brought the opera to life.

I am closer to the stage – no strain to see (I have poor eyesight).

The third of these links enjoyment of close-ups with other ways in which this person felt she was brought close to the performance – the access to, and insights from, an opera's producers. This sense of closeness outruns achieved physical proximity, as in another respondent's list of appreciated qualities: 'closeness to the action, backstage ambiance, interviews with actors'. These combine to give a heightened sense of participation for many people.

Beyond these important and most obvious points, other things are also at work. If ambivalence towards Alternative Content is marked by that use of 'Obviously … but' construction, the other side of this coin is often characterized by a small but significant variation on this: the use of words such as 'surprisingly', 'strangely', and 'weirdly', as in these answers to my 'liveness' question:

> Very like, surprisingly so, and almost as good. Presumably because one is seeing it as it happens (or at least almost as it happens) and knows that gaffes, unforeseen problems, etc., cannot be corrected or air-brushed out as in recorded or filmed events, therefore there is a sense of danger. Since no performance can ever be completely like another there is also a sense of completion. No-one who was not there will ever be able to have exactly that experience.

> Larger than life … surprisingly intimate, great visibility, and interesting introductions.

> Strangely more absorbing, because camera operator expertise presents a huge variety of shots and engages the concentration more deeply in the performance.

> Having attended the Metropolitan Opera in New York many times (in fact, I attended during one of the live broadcasts last year), I find the experience more intense and gripping at the cinema. The Met is such a huge and cavernous space that I felt very little connection with what was happening on stage. On the cinema screen, being able to see the faces of the singers and registering the emotions they convey offers a far better experience. The sound in the multiplexes is also surprisingly more vibrant and involving than a live set-up. In addition I find the UK cinema audiences at these events far more attentive and better behaved than the American audiences at the Met where talking, eating and fidgeting can prove extremely annoying.

> Better, because you're practically there on stage with the singers, rather than seeing them from some distance in a live theatre. You do however miss the immediate excitement of a live performance and being in the presence of great artists, but surprisingly this is no big deal. Also I'd never be able to afford to go to a dozen operas of this quality in a season anyway, so each one is a bonus.

The significance of this surely is that people within this orientation to Alternative Content *assumed* that they could not be like the originating event, but – having savoured them – found them greatly to their liking, and even an improvement on being at source. These events went against expectations – and, of course, that was particularly possible because for many people these were novel experiences. First, or second, visits to these screenings meant that people were *still learning* what they could offer. For some, therefore, this sense of surprise and discovery linked with awareness of not being sure about appropriate 'audience manners', as here:

> It's better than any seat in the house. The only slightly weird thing is that everyone feels they want to applaud the best things but it is silly to applaud a cinema screen.

This is because for people such as this the cinema screen became *permeable*. The controlled camerawork and sound provision made the experience more *direct*. Emphasis in a number of answers on the *sense of closeness* that people experienced marks this transparency of the screen.

The implications of 'closeness'

In fact, the idea of 'closeness' provides a key discursive marker within my whole database of responses. Among the 639 responses, more than half spontaneously used the word at some point in giving those two answers. Unsurprisingly, a large proportion of these are direct mentions of the use of close-ups. But even with these it is easy to determine what attitudes people were taking to them. Coding for Positive (for instance, 'Better for seeing close-up'), Ambivalent ('Close-ups can be good but sometimes the whole stage view is better') and Negative ('Disconcerting seeing singers so close up') in association with ratings of the experience produces Table 2.2:

Table 2.2

	1–2 Ratings	3–5 Ratings
Positive	63.1%	15.4%
Ambivalent	28.4%	36.6%
Negative	8.5%	50.0%
Mentions[5]	336	26

For Negatives, close-ups are sources of discomfort and irritation. They inappropriately reveal the age of performers and take you too close to flawed faces – with broader costs ('the close-ups of singers are not always attractive and make it difficult to suspend belief'). They prevent you attending to interactions between performers ('concentration on close-ups detracted from an appreciation of the interaction of the performers with each other'). They remind people of television programmes and values ('The direction should portray the theatrical performance and atmosphere NOT try to create a TV or film version with close-ups'). And – perhaps more than any other – they take away audiences' control over the process of looking. Now, the camera is determining where you can look – and that is disapproved of. One example well captures what is implied by this:

> Such a viewing cannot really compare with being in the actual theatre as you are obliged to look at what the camera sees and not where you might wish to look. In addition close-ups of singers/actors which cannot happen when viewing in the theatre can occasionally destroy the illusion that is built up by distance.

Here again 'closeness' is experienced as a threat to this kind of controlled viewing with its 'managed illusion'. This appears to be the emergent critique of those who, even if they appreciated the opportunity to see events they otherwise had no chance of accessing, still felt a clear loss of something very important to them. By contrast, a quite different orientation emerges from close examination of those who welcomed and appreciated close-ups. This could of course contain that benefit to challenged eyesight or simple distance from events from being in cheap seats. But a considerable number of those use the word 'close' approvingly to mean and imply much more. A total of 78 answers from among those giving the more positive ratings reveal some large expansions of the word's meaning, as in these examples:

> As in many cinema screenings I was able to feel part of the story but with the extra close-ups I could feel and enter into the real emotions being expressed. In films the acting of emotion is often too obvious. At an actual opera the audience can detract from what is happening on stage. In this performance the focus was on the stage itself, which was better.

> The music and accessibility to the performers was wonderful, you would not get this close a view on stage. Seeing the interviews and backstage was excellent; again, not something you would experience at the theatre.

> Although I have seen several operas live on stage and live or as live on television, I prefer this method of delivery – close-up shots of the principals that help to drive the narrative. The big screen is a definite bonus. It's more social than a live performance in that – united by a common experience – you are more likely to talk to other members of the audience.

> Better – got closer and the behind the scenes stuff is excellent – a good educational experience.

> It seems less distracting to have the subtitles on the screen close to what one is watching rather than surtitles above the stage – this makes the story more immediate somehow.

It is better because you get close up to the performers. I also think that the performers up their performance because they are aware that they will be seen really close up.

Seeing it in closeup (when the director got the right shot – which was most of the time) meant that you could understand more of the play, the characters and the interactions between them. Because the cameras were being controlled by someone who knew the play better than me (I assume) you were helped by having your attention focussed.

It is of course risky to presume that any individuals will adopt and share this entire set of judgements. Nonetheless, it is revealing to draw all these aspects together, and think about the ways in which they may throw light on the repeated use of words such as 'contact', 'involvement' and 'intimacy' to capture people's positive responses (ideas that were captured non-discursively in NESTA's 2009 research). We might view the results as constituting an *ideal-type*, that is, what a fully developed version of this emergent phenomenon might look like. The quotations above unpack 'closeness' to mean all the following: access to performers' emotions and interactions; the elimination of interference from other audience members; yet the creation in the same process of a new sense of communality of experience; a sense of privileged access to performers, designers and directors as well as the production itself; an intensified sense that performers are doing their best, for you; and the constitution of the whole event as an *emotional learning experience* in which one could be guided by others who know more and can introduce and 'educate' you in otherwise difficult materials. In all this, camerawork at its best is not a mediation but a special mode of access.[6] Most importantly, people are identifying this as 'live' in new, even increased senses, as here:

A different experience but in a way better because you are so close to the action. The cinema was comfortable and the view was unrestricted. The view of the New York audience and the interviews with the performers reminded you that it was a live event so it didn't feel the same as watching a recording of a previous performance.

An increasing attraction is that the opera screenings are attended by many of my neighbours so a party atmosphere is building up.

Of course, like any other event, it can go wrong, and people reserve the right to criticize particular aspects, whether technical (breaks in transmission, wrong sound levels and the like) or aesthetic (bad choices of camera angles or overactive editing). But a sense shows among respondents of a new *kind* of event, requiring different manners. These cover *applause* (a number remark on their uncertainty about clapping, then relief when they realize that they can – and how they realize they are partly clapping *to inform each other* of their enjoyment), *audience manners* (dislike of people complaining, welcome for fellow enthusiasts), *well-chosen additional materials* (good and involved interviewers, guiding programme notes, entertaining shots of the live audience), *relaxed and unpretentious atmosphere* (one irritated respondent commented on this: 'Unfortunately at my cinema the audience seems probably to be mostly composed of third rate academics, local Government bods and others who have had a cushioned life-style. They are all so uptight and refuse to clap at the big moments and join in the experience. I think academics in particular should be charged double and then they might appreciate what is on offer'), and a *willing giving over of control to those whom you trust with the experience.*[7]

I have called this an ideal-typical description of something emergent. The sense of its novelty is shown in small ways in many of the answers, but is made quite explicit in these:

It takes a little time to get used to the close-ups, a different way of seeing opera.

At the beginning it was a bit annoying that I couldn't see the entire stage all the time but I got used to this much more quickly than I thought I would and enjoyed the performance from this new perspective having my view chosen for me.

It is great to be able to see at very close quarters the happenings and characters on stage – and to really get into their skins. The only thing that detracts for me is not being able to let go and voice my enthusiasms when applicable. Very difficult staying mute/dumb when all around you show no emotion!!

It was so like being at the event that I forgot I was at the cinema and clapped when the theatre audience clapped.

Audience participation is odd; to clap or not to clap, for instance.

Better view, better price, the addition of the interesting interviews make this experience preferable. There was a feeling of liveness so much so that I wanted to clap but felt a bit silly doing so. I missed this – the opportunity to respond with applause to performers who could hear that applause. I liked the intervals with drinks just as at the event itself for the opportunity of relaxing and chatting with others about the performance in progress.

It is evident that right to applaud is one of the markers for many people of an event's 'liveness' to them. That is, of course, a challenging notion since it is known that some audiences will applaud films.

Conclusions

A considerable body of recent research has sought to identify the intrinsic benefits of the arts to its audiences (Brown & Novak 2007; Radbourne et al. 2010). This is of course partly because new funding regimes have increased pressures on cultural producers to prove the benefits of their provision. But the downside of this is that the more commercially oriented such research is, the more it will tend to stop short of asking about the broader cultural implications of the engagements it identifies. Because the primary motive is simply to attract and hold audiences, the nature of their pleasures can be taken as given. What my research has tried to do is to unpack the nature of these, to explore their nature and operations.

Within British culture and much more widely, the idea of 'liveness' has long carried an imprimatur of value and validity, with consequent awarding of lower value, if not critical distrust, of the 'non-live'. What I believe my research shows is that 'liveness' is a complex phenomenon, with many separable components. However much this may frustrate those who invest heavily in their preferred model of this liveness, audiences are capable of picking and choosing which ones matter to them. Some of these do not relate to physical presence at the performance itself, but to other ways an audience may collectively encounter it. Both providers and audiences, meanwhile, have to learn how they are entitled and supposed to engage with these new kinds of 'liveness'. That process is still underway. If the period 2006–10 was the experimental period in which novelty was perhaps a prime value in Alternative Content, now, with maturity, is coming some confidence. Of course, along with that will go new critical criteria – is *this* 'live' performance as well presented as previous encounters? We have yet to see, to my knowledge, any specialist regimes of review and critical exchange, but they will surely come. Professional training programmes for producers and broadcasters of these events have yet to emerge. The future of these events is pretty rosy. It is time for arts researchers to catch up.

There is at least one other major implication arising from this development, and the research associated with it. This concerns the debates on the issues of 'univores' and 'omnivores'. Peterson and colleagues (Peterson & Simkus 1992; Peterson & Kern 1996) introduced the concept of the omnivore with their critiques of Pierre Bourdieu's views on the taste preferences of highbrow consumers. They claimed to show that, whether or not it was true in 1960s France, today, at least in America, a highbrow orientation is characterized by willingness to enjoy all kinds of culture. This research has proved both influential and controversial. While Bennett et al. (1999) claimed in large measure to substantiate his claims in their research on Australian taste cultures, others have challenged his findings. Chan and Goldthorpe (2005), for instance, explored the responses to a major survey by the UK Arts Council, and concluded not only that taste cultures remain connected (albeit in complicated ways) with class and status, but also that some taste preferences more precisely relate to social inequality than others. And Warde et al. (2007), drawing on both survey and interview materials, conclude that 'we should be very suspicious of the notion of *the* omnivore as a characterization or ideal type of cultural actor' (2007: 160).

What the emerging research on Alternative Content indicates is two things. First, engagement with those art forms tending to be associated with a highbrow orientation is uneven. It is not necessarily the same audiences who will attend opera, theatre, and dance performances. This emerges clearly from various quantitative surveys, including my own. But secondly, and perhaps more importantly, there are clear indications that enthusiasts' *manner of engaging* with each of these – how selective they are, what critical criteria they bring to bear, and so on – may not coincide. Indeed, the differences and conflicts I encountered among audiences over 'how to watch' suggest that attendance alone is not enough to settle the arguments between Bourdieu's notion of the 'distanced' highbrow viewer, and Peterson's generalized omnivore.

References

Auslander, P. (1999), *Liveness*, London: Routledge.

Barker, M. & Brooks, K. (1997), *Knowing Audiences: Judge Dredd, its Friends, Fans and Foes*, Luton: University of Luton Press.

Barker, M. & Mathijs, E. (eds) (2007), *Watching The Lord of the Rings*, New York: Peter Lang.

Belsey, C. (1998), 'Shakespeare and Film: a Question of Perspective', in R. Shaughnessy (ed.), *Shakespeare on Film*, Basingstoke: Macmillan, pp. 61–70.

Bennett, T., Emmison, M. & Frow, J. (1999), *Accounting for Tastes: Australian Everyday Cultures*, Cambridge: Cambridge University Press.

Bourdon, J. (2000), 'Live Television is Still Alive: On Television as an Unfulfilled Promise', *Media, Culture & Society*, 22: 5, pp. 531–66.

Brown, A.S. & Novak, J.L. (2007), *Assessing the Intrinsic Impacts of a Live Performance*, WolfBrown, http://www.wolfbrown.com/mups_downloads/Impact_Study_Final_Version_full.pdf. (accessed 27 March 2011).

Chan, T.W. & Goldthorpe, J. H. (2005), 'The Social Stratification of Theatre, Dance and Cinema Attendance', *Cultural Trends*, 14: 3, pp. 193–212.

Crawford, G. (2009), 'Consuming Sport, Consuming Beer: Sport Fans, Scene and Everyday Life', in L.A. Wenner & S.J. Jackson (eds) *Sport, Beer, and Gender: Promotional Culture & Contemporary Social Life*, New York: Peter Lang Publishing, pp. 279–98.

Croft, J. (2007), 'Theses on Liveness', *Organized Sound*, 12: 1, pp. 59–66.

Ellis, J. (1982), *Visible Fictions*, London: Routledge, Kegan & Paul.

Feuer, J (1983), 'The Concept of Live Television: Ontology as Ideology', in E.A. Kaplan (ed.) *Regarding Television*, Los Angeles: American Film Institute, pp. 12–22.

Hare, D. (2009), 'The Decade of Looking Away', *Guardian Weekend*, 17 October, pp. 5–7.

Heyer, P. (2008), 'Live from the Met: Digital Broadcast Cinema, Medium Theory, and Opera for the Masses', *Canadian Journal of Communication*, 33: 4, pp. 591–604.

Jones, C., & Hancock, D. (2009), 'Alternative Content in Cinemas: Market Assessment and Forecasts to 2014', *Screen Digest Report*.

Keyishian, H. (2008), 'Film as Performance: Cinematized Shakespeare', in F. Occhiogrosso (ed.) *Shakespearean Performance: New Studies*, Madison: Fairleigh Dickinson, pp. 50–61.

Koven, M. J. (2008), *Film, Folklore and Urban Legends*, Lanham, MD: Scarecrow Press.

Palmer, D. (2000), 'Webcams: The Aesthetics of Liveness', *LIKE, Art Magazine*, 12 (Winter), pp. 16–22.

Phelan, P. (1993), *Unmarked: the Politics of Performance*, London: Routledge.

Radbourne, J., Johanson, K., & Glow, H. (2010), 'Empowering Audiences to Measure Quality', *Participations*, 7: 2, pp. 360–79.

Scarpetta, F. & Spagnolli, A. (2009), 'The Interactional Context of Humour in Stand-up Comedy', *Research on Language and Social Interaction*, 42: 3, pp. 210–30.

Warde, A., Wright, D. & Gayo-Cal, M. (2007), 'Understanding Cultural Omnivorousness: Or, the Myth of the Cultural Omnivore', *Cultural Sociology*, 1: 2, pp. 143–64.

Weed, M. (2007), 'The Pub as a Virtual Football Fandom Venue: An Alternative to "Being There"?', *Soccer and Society*, 8: 2, pp. 399–414.

Notes

1   Up until 2011, ballet has been less successful than theatre and opera, partly because its audience is more specialized than the other art forms. In an attempt to overcome this, one of the second-wave start-up distributors, More2Screen, announced the 'world's first ballet in 3D': *Giselle* from the renowned Mariinsky Theatre in St Petersburg. More2Screen's own attendance figures suggest average audiences of just over 50 per cinema – hardly a startling breakthrough.

2   As far as I have been able to tell, explorations of the concept and its issues are almost entirely absent from some other fields where you might have expected it to operate: music and dance studies, for instance. For a rare exception, see Croft 2007.

3   I have to record my gratitude to Picturehouse not only for enabling my research, but for allowing me access to their own data, in a form which allowed me to reanalyse them, and discover further things. For instance, reanalysis of their data on the New York Met screenings showed an association between age and appreciation of the event. This group also turns out to be markedly more interested in attending other events – even when they are pre-recorded. My hunch is that this marks an older population's interest in having a wide range of cultural activities to hand, now that they are in retirement.

4   All these quotations are taken from anonymized responses to my survey. In some cases where meaning was evident and for ease of reading here, I have tidied spelling or punctuation, out of courtesy to my respondents who may well have completed the survey in a hurry. My thanks to all those who responded to my request.

5   The imbalance of total numbers here partly reflects a greater willingness of more positive respondents to mention 'closeness'. It is of course partly due to the fact that, at the point where I did my research, general levels of enthusiasm were high, therefore my sample was not 'balanced' in this respect.

6   Sadly, in the one other piece of academic writing I have so far located on this area, Paul Heyer – in an otherwise enterprising early study of the New York Met's broadcasts – falls straight into the film theory trap of trying to deploy theories of 'voyeurism': 'Close-ups can render the performers larger than life, as if on a movie screen. The gaze is crucial, since attention is usually riveted on the performers, especially in productions such as Gounod's *Roméo et Juliette* (15 December 2007) where the two leads were riveted on each other.

The tenets of voyeurism and its associated pleasures as elaborated in film theory inspired by psychoanalysis (Mulvey 1985) likewise have applicability' (2008, this quote, p. 599). Their 'applicability' is precisely what should be at issue here.

7 This final aspect can include some surprising elements. The manager of Aberystwyth Arts Centre Cinema told me of his experience in running these events. He has developed a practice of speaking briefly to patrons before each event, introducing what will happen. For this, he breaks his normal habit of very casual dress and wears shirt and tie. On two occasions he happened to be away, and he heard on his return of complaints that the event had been unsatisfactory because he had not been there to guide them appropriately into it.

Chapter 3

Challenging Cultural Authority: A Case Study in Participative Audience Engagement

Hilary Glow

From 2010–2012 the Theatre Royal Stratford East (TRSE) in East London is engaging in a project called Open Stage. Using community volunteers as cultural intermediaries, the project is focused on building community engagement culminating in a co-curated season of performance works in 2012. This chapter is a case study of the Open Stage project; it outlines the organization's community engagement process, and interrogates the reasons why such work is significant and timely.

The rationales and purposes of community engagement for arts organizations are shaped by two primary influences; the relatively new focus of arts marketing on the relationship between consumption and co-creation; and the political and cultural imperatives around social inclusion. The case study investigated here suggests that there are synergies between these two forces in the sense that both emphasize the need for arts organizations to shake off their traditional definition as mediators of 'legitimate' culture and knowledge. The TRSE's Open Stage is an exemplar of this shift in priority; it represents a significant move away from the conventionally patrician and elitist role of the arts organization as the arbiter of culture, towards a new role in facilitating active community participation and responding to the diverse publics and communities it serves.

Beyond the challenge to arts organizations, there is a broader socio-cultural need. Many groups with an expressed social and political commitment to building social cohesion do so in recognition of the increasingly fragmented nature of individual lives. In the workplace, the neighbourhood and the street we experience what Zygmunt Bauman calls 'the increasing frailty of human bonds' (2008: 38). In heterogeneous communities – like East London where TRSE is situated – which are distinguished by a great diversity of languages, experiences and histories, there is a task of empowerment to be continuously confronted. Bauman points out that the skills we need more than any others in order to offer the public sphere 'a reasonable chance of resuscitation' are the skills of 'interaction with others – of conducting a dialogue, of negotiating, of gaining mutual understanding, and of managing or resolving the conflicts inevitable in every instance of shared life' (2008: 190).

In 2009 Ben Cameron, program director of the US's Doris Duke Charitable Foundation, called for arts practitioners, managers, advocates, marketers and policy makers to question the notion of 'cultural authority'; to critically examine who gets to set the cultural agenda and why. The democratization of both artistic production and the means of artistic distribution has catalysed a redefinition of authorship and the cultural market. Cameron writes: 'Today everyone is a potential author – and the market paradigm is shifting from one of traditional consumption to one of participation. In the future, value will not be consumed: value will be co-created' (2009).

How performing arts organizations respond to the challenge of co-creation is a complex question and requires new ways of thinking about not just the presentation of works, but audience engagement and enhanced opportunities for interaction. Audiences want to interact with the creative process and not just the end product.

The TRSE has a distinguished history of audience engagement. Under the current artistic directorship of Kerry Michael, audiences and volunteers from the community will become co-curators in determining the work of the company in 2012. Such activities can be seen to be informed by both the general policy environment with its interest in the arts as a means for social inclusion and the new arts marketing discourse with its focus on audience engagement. Open Stage is of particular interest for its deployment of community volunteers as cultural intermediaries. It is argued here that the TRSE has taken up the challenge of audience engagement through the development of co-curatorial relationships with community members and that this participative approach to the task of setting the cultural agenda represents a radical shift in traditional notions of cultural authority.

The notion of the 'cultural intermediary' originally comes from Bordieu, who identifies how familiarity with high culture is a scarce resource distributed along class lines. Bourdieu uses the term 'cultural intermediary' to identify a group of middle-class professionals working for institutions 'providing symbolic goods and services', in occupations such as marketing, sales, public relations, fashion and decoration (2000: 359). Their intermediary status is a function of their capacity to bridge – to appreciate and consume – both high and popular arts and thereby to blur traditional definitions of these activities. More recent scholarship has seen the role of cultural intermediaries as one of 'providing a bridge between the market and culture' (Durrer & Miles 2009: 229); or as shaping 'both use values and exchange values' and managing how these values are 'connected with people's lives through the various techniques of persuasion' (Negus 2002: 504).

Kurin (1997) notes that museums have long been concerned with the issue of public cultural representation; the issue, that is, of 'who is saying what about whom?' (1997: 13). As an example of this, Ross (2004) identifies a 'new museology' that has come about as a result of museum professionals becoming increasingly aware of their role, not as definers of legitimate culture, but as interpreters with a 'heightened awareness of diverse audiences and publics, a commitment to facilitating wider access ... and to the mediation of social difference' (2004: 90). For Kurin, in the context of cultural representation, the notion of cultural 'brokerage' is useful in that it defines a role for museum and curatorial personnel in 'active, respectful engagement' to bring together audiences with the institution (1997: 23). Kurin sees the emergence of a professional role in museums for 'technicians of the liminal': museum staff 'skilled at enabling transitions ... and satisfying the needs of the parties involved' (1997: 21).

Negus (2002), *pace* Bourdieu, uses the notion of 'cultural intermediaries' to define a role that comes in-between creative artists and consumers and whose work signals a shift away from transmission models of cultural production towards an approach whereby 'intermediaries [are] continually engaged in forming a point of connection or articulation between production and consumption' (2002: 503). Negus provides a critique of those interpretations of the role of cultural intermediaries, which (as with Kurin's notion of the cultural broker) privilege a particular cluster of occupations and which 'accord certain workers a pivotal role in these processes of symbolic mediation, prioritizing a narrow and reductionist aesthetic' (2002: 504).

Why must we exist today?

In his speech, subtitled 'Arts in the 21st Century', Cameron suggests that arts organizations need to ask themselves a primary question: 'Why must we exist today?' It is primary because no other consideration really matters in establishing a raison d'être: not the existence of buildings that house arts organizations, not their histories, infrastructures, awards or reputations.

Cameron argues that for arts organizations to survive into the twenty-first century they will need to re-think their relationships with their communities and be able to answer three questions:

- What is the value my organization brings to my community?
- What is the value my organization alone brings or brings better than anyone else?
- How would my community be damaged if we closed our doors and went away tomorrow?

If arts organizations cannot answer these questions, Cameron argues, 'the only supporters we are likely to find already sit in our seats' (2009).

The pressing need to ask (and find answers to) these difficult questions has arisen particularly in the light of the global financial crisis, which has occasioned general consumer anxiety and declining discretionary income. The economic downturn leads Cameron to speculate that (in the United States, at least) there will be a decline in audience attendance across the performing arts (Cameron 2009). In addition, the level of government support for arts organizations, along with donations from philanthropic, corporate and individual sponsors, are all decreasing.

The challenge to arts organizations posed by Cameron is not simply one of developing more sophisticated marketing techniques, but of redefining and re-visioning the nature of the cultural task. Arts organizations cannot afford to continue to think of themselves as producers or presenters of cultural product, rather they are the 'orchestrators of social interaction' with communities who are seeking opportunities for interactivity, participation, access and engagement. The preference for active modes of engagement by audiences (and potential audiences) represents, Cameron argues, an assault on our traditional notions of cultural authority and the 'assumed ability of traditional arts organizations to set the cultural agenda' (2009).

In this context it is interesting to look at the TRSE's Open Stage project; a project dedicated to democratizing theatre; to listening to the voices and stories of those in the community that are not often heard; and to building a sense of empowerment and ownership of the theatre by the local community. This process of empowering audiences involves what the artistic director Kerry Michael refers to as 'giving up our power' by 'sharing it with people who want to come along to that party' (Michael Interview 2011). By turning to their community and asking them what they want to see in the theatre, the TRSE are turning on its head the traditional cultural authority of the arts organization and the role of its creative leadership.

Open Stage: Theatre Royal Stratford East

The TRSE began its life in 1953 as a political theatre collective called the Theatre Workshop, under the artistic directorship of Joan Littlewood. Dedicated to producing theatre for the working class, the TRSE repudiated the middle-class monopoly of theatre, and sought to produce popular politically informed plays under the banner: 'The great theatres of all time have been popular theatres which reflected the dramas and struggles of the people' (quoted in Eyre & Wright 2000: 261). For Littlewood, a 'popular' theatre was one that reached non-metropolitan and non-middle class audiences and sought to inform and entertain them.

The TRSE continues to demonstrate a commitment to producing theatre work that 'reflects the concerns, hopes and dreams of the people of East London' (TRSE 2008 Annual Report). East London's Newham Borough has a large immigrant community with over 100 languages spoken, and is London's youngest borough with a youth population of 68 per cent (TRSE 2009–10 Annual Report). Under the artistic directorship of Kerry Michael the company has dedicated itself to 'giving voice to stories rarely heard'; to developing young talent (including writers, directors and performers); and to producing new work that reflects the cultural diversity of the community (2008: 7).

In an extension of the company's long commitment to a community-centred approach, the theatre launched its Open Stage project in 2010, a two-year initiative designed to hand programming control over to the public to determine what will appear at the venue in the lead up to the London Olympic and Paralympic Games in 2012. The Open Stage project aims to 'research, devise, deliver and evaluate a new model of public engagement' through dialogue, the embedding of partnerships with local people and the empowerment of new audiences (Handel 2010).

In an interview with the author, artistic director Kerry Michael identified a number of key motivations for the Open Stage project. First, he explained that with the announcement of the 2012 London Olympics there were a number of public assurances that the Cultural Olympiad would 'belong to everybody'; a promise, he says, that hasn't quite materialized. As a major arts organization with the closest proximity to the Games, Michael and his team felt that they needed a project that would 'empower our community … to have some ownership of culture during [the Olympics]'. Second, the TRSE is keen to build and extend its community outreach work, 'our conversations with the community', so that once the Olympics is over there is a better understanding of its impact. While community engagement is a long-standing priority of the company, there is a need to 'put extra effort' into building community connection and outreach for the period following the Games, particularly in the light of the changing demographics of East London. Third, Open Stage has been designed to 'test the organization's DNA'. Michael sought to review the assumptions and practices of the TRSE; to 'not rest on our laurels' as an organization already well-known for its audience engagement:

> If you keep doing the same thing in the same way, actually how do you know it still works, and how do you know it's the right way of doing things? By doing this program we have to deconstruct all that shorthand and we have to explain it again … and just remind ourselves of what we're doing.

Finally, and confluent with Cameron's call for arts organizations to question established notions of cultural authority, Michael identified the need to provoke debate about the role of arts organizations and their publics: 'I wanted to do something that was big enough and significant enough [to cause] debate amongst our peers and our funding bodies and our sector, about who's here for whom? Who's here to serve whom? Who's our paymaster?' (Michael Interview 2011).

What would you like to see in Open Stage?

Open Stage began with the theatre company recruiting 25 'co-programmers'; volunteers from the community whose jobs were to develop relationships with local residents. Volunteers were cross-generational and from diverse ethnic backgrounds, reflecting the diversity of the East London community. They were recruited through a range of channels including the theatre company's website and email list, community and volunteer organization contacts and word of mouth. Once recruited, the team of volunteers engaged in a training process to develop skills including interview and communication techniques and administering questionnaires that were drafted with input from the staff of the TRSE (Handel Interview 2011).

On the pilot weekend, the team of volunteers went out into the streets of Stratford in pairs to interview the public. Interviews took place in commuter and shopping areas, the library, bus stations, cafes, bars and in the mall. A total of 229 people were interviewed (from a range of ages and ethnic backgrounds) and were asked a number of questions about their awareness of, and interest in, the work of the theatre. Fifty per cent of those interviewed had not previously been to the TRSE, and 50 per cent had visited the bar in the theatre building (to eat and drink), or had seen free events in the bar, or had been to a show. In particular, respondents were asked, 'What would you like to see in Open Stage?' Once people had been interviewed in the street they were invited to come into the building, to meet the volunteers and the staff of the organization (Handel Interview 2011).

The information gathered through this exercise related to the volunteer experience, the TRSE staff experience, and the responses of interviewees. The volunteers reported a high level of engagement in the process; all agreed to continue to be involved in the project and more volunteers subsequently signed up. Volunteers expressed a variety of motivations for their participation: some wanted to take on the responsibility for programming the season, some were interested in developing their knowledge and skills in production areas such as stage management, and others were interested in producing blogs, working on promotion, audience research and data analysis (Handel Interview 2011).

The excitement generated by the process also had the effect of encouraging TRSE staff to take ownership and build their active engagement in the project. Out of 33 staff members, 15 staff volunteered their time to take part. They reported that spending time with the project volunteers was the 'highlight' of the experience. The feedback from staff generated an understanding of the importance of building the sense of ownership of the building for the project volunteers.

The responses of interviewees delivered some very specific information about topics of shows they'd like to see; but generally the feedback was in the form of suggestions of genres people wanted to see on stage: pantomimes, real-life stories, comedy and musicals were the most frequently mentioned. Of the 229 people interviewed 100 wanted to find out more about TRSE; and 25 per cent of those interviewed wanted to find out more or be involved in the Open Stage project.

Following the pilot stage, a website was developed so that the 'conversations' that had begun with community members, and between the TRSE staff, volunteers and the public could continue online. The Open Stage website invites people to participate (also via blogs, Twitter, Facebook) to contribute ideas and to interact with the volunteers. The website explains that all ideas are welcome with a caveat: 'There are three rules about what will be programmed: the project must change the organization in some way; it can't bankrupt the theatre and we won't put anything on stage that will incite hatred' (Open Stage 2011).

From September 2010 to September 2011 volunteers and staff asked over 1500 people for their views on what they would like to see. In May 2011 the volunteers entered a phase of training in programming with the intention of using their research to curate a six-month season of works from January to July 2012. Their professional development (while not strictly speaking a training program) used TRSE staff to mentor volunteers by showing them the processes of casting actors, licensing script rights, script development and collaboration with artists. In addition, facilitated sessions addressed decision-making processes, working as a team and project planning.

Specifically, the volunteers addressed the complexities of programming through skill development sessions with the artistic director, Kerry Michael. This involved a critical interrogation of the genre of musicals as this had been the most frequently suggested programming option that emerged through the consultation process. At the same time, volunteers considered a range of operational issues such as budget and financial resources, facilities, target audiences, selling point and scheduling.

The TRSE is not alone in exploring forms of community participation. Other projects in the United Kingdom include, for example, the National Theatre of Wales, which, in collaboration with Wildworks, produced a contemporary and community-based version of *The Passion* over an Easter weekend in 2011 in Port Talbot, South Wales. Combining professional actors and musicians with local participants involved as cast and crew, and using contemporary stories and various spaces and locales for the setting, the production was developed with the participation of over 1,000 volunteers, and the final production attracted 22,000 people in the town to watch the performance. The production 'was like watching a town discovering its voice through a shared act of creation' (Gardiner 2011). The National Theatre of Wales, like TRSE, has been focused on audience engagement as a primary task; the concern is for producing work that is participatory, topical, innovative, welcomed by the community, ethical and leaves a valuable legacy. In their mission, they undertake that 'community engagement and participation will be a feature of every single piece of work we make' (National Theatre of Wales 2011).

In the UK, community-based and participative performance work has received a sizable boost with the announcement in 2011 of the Gulbenkian award. The award, a £175,000 art prize, funded by the Calouste Gulbenkian Foundation, supports the development of a new performance piece in which leading professionals work with disadvantaged communities. The aim is to produce works that are involving and innovative, and reflect 'uncompromisingly high artistic standards' (Calouste Gulbenkian Foundation 2011).

Under consideration for the award are projects from the National Theatre of Scotland, the Birmingham Opera Company, the National Theatre of Wales and The Young Vic, which is producing a new work – *Beijing Bicycle*. Based in the theatre's neighbourhood (near Waterloo station in London) and inspired by the classic Chinese film, this is a large-scale theatre piece to be performed both on stage and on bikes outside the theatre, involving actors, cyclists and members of the local community (Tait 2011).

Arts marketing meets social inclusion

In the UK, at least, the development of community-based and participatory theatre practices has to be seen in the light of the stated priority of the previous Labour government to promote socially engaged work. Indeed, this cultural priority continues to hold sway or to have an ideological basis in the current Conservative government's focus on the notion of 'the big society' and the role of volunteering. Social exclusion is a stated issue of concern in UK public policy and is directed at 'people or areas fac[ing] a combination of linked problems such as unemployment, discrimination, poor skills, low incomes, poor housing, high crime'

(Department for Work and Pensions 2008–2010). At the same time, the Department of Culture, Media and Sport (DCMS) has argued that engagement in the arts has direct social benefits for participants including increased self-esteem leading to greater opportunities for employment, skill development and networking (2007).

The Gulbenkian award also promotes participatory art works on the basis of their 'demonstrable social benefits', and at the same time the development of audience-focused cultural practices is widely reinforced through new discourses within arts marketing. Cameron, quoted at the beginning of this chapter, along with others such as Walker-Kuhn, promote the notion of audience development not as a way of ameliorating social problems, but as a matter of engaging diverse audiences in a creative process. Such thinking within the field of arts marketing represents a shift from a customer-centred and service provision approach towards, what Boorsma calls, 'the co-production of artistic value' (2006: 76). Boorsma argues that this new arts marketing 'logic' requires arts organizations to 'equally respect the roles of artists and arts consumers in the total art process' and to develop an orientation towards 'the co-creative capabilities of customers' (2006: 87).

One of the significant features of the Open Stage project at the TRSE is that in some respects it embodies the shift away from the notion of service provision to the 'total art process' identified by Boorsma. The shift involves a whole-of-organization approach; Charlotte Handel, the project manager of Open Stage noted that:

> What's changing is the view of who is responsible for this kind of work, going out and talking to the community … It used to be seen [by theatre companies] as the responsibility of your education department, and then it moved into the marketing department. But for us it's about the whole building … everybody is involved in this work. Actually, my idea is that at the end of the process there won't be a job for me because everyone will be doing it so well, and [the company] will have such good advocates in the community, and they'll feel so connected, they won't need somebody to mediate their relationships.
>
> (Handel Interview 2011)

In this sense the Open Stage project can be seen to be informed by both the general policy environment with its concern for the relationship between arts and social inclusion, and the new discourse within arts marketing with its focus on audience experience and engagement. Durrer and Miles (2009: 225) argue that these two forces are inter-connected – that marketing for arts institutions, dedicated to attracting wider audiences, is an explicit response to 'the social inclusion agenda within British cultural policy'. In their study of UK arts managers working for institutions that address 'socially excluded' audiences, Durrer and Miles found that new approaches to marketing depend on 'a personalized approach that promotes dialogue, trust and relationship building and is maintained by … gatekeepers entrusted with the task of attracting "socially excluded" individuals into arts institutions' (2009: 226).

The Open Stage project is still current, and the results (in terms of the six-month season of theatre works) will be on display in 2012. However, for the purposes of this chapter, it is the process itself which is significant, and in particular the development of the role of the volunteers as cultural gatekeepers or intermediaries.

Volunteer as cultural intermediary

One of the key features of the TRSE Open Stage is the way in which the role of community volunteer is being developed into the role of cultural intermediary. As Kurin's definition allows, they are cultural brokers in the sense that they are bringing audiences to the institution. But their role is not confined to either the arena of production or consumption but exists 'at the point where production and consumption articulate' (Negus 2002: 513). Their status as community members and volunteers is an important part of their mediating role. Durrer and Miles' study identifies the role played by arts managers as cultural intermediaries working with excluded audiences – particularly those working in education and outreach programs – but make the point that 'from their positions … these cultural intermediaries are able to exercise certain amounts of cultural authority over audiences of socially excluded individuals, thus still serving as shapers of taste' (2009: 230). In the case of Open Stage, the intermediary role is one of co-curation; the volunteers are forming links with socially excluded individuals, providing access for those individuals to the institution and helping to shape the artistic product that emerges as a result of the mediation process. They are, in other words, participants in the creative process seeking a level of engagement with the theatre company that is informed, active, reflexive and empowered.

Durrer and Miles' findings suggest that the positional power (the 'institutional seniority') of the cultural intermediary influences the manner in which the organization's social inclusion policy is delivered; the organizational position of this role matters because it determines 'the extent to which he or she reinforces a definition of the arts that is inherently elitist' (2009: 239). However, where the role of cultural intermediary is played by community volunteers whose professional skill development is supported by the whole of the theatre company, the social inclusion outcomes become embedded in the work of the organization. The conceptualization of these volunteers as co-curators of the 2012 season means that they are shaping the artistic product in a way that blurs the conventional dichotomy between cultural producers and consumers, and can be seen as an exemplar of a participative approach to setting the cultural agenda.

Challenging cultural authority

Leadbeater (2009) describes how, in a commoditized world, organizations tend to do things *to* and *for* people based on a number of deeply rooted assumptions: 'Knowledge and learning flows from experts to people who are dependent or in need. Organizations are hierarchies based on the power and the knowledge to make decisions. Authority is exercised top down. The aim is to define what people lack – what they need or want that they have not got – and then deliver it to them' (2009: 3). In Leadbeater's admittedly generalized account of the way artists and cultural organizations tend to work, the artist is often seen as working in a field marked by 'separation and specialism' that apparently allows an un-co-opted and 'uncompromising vantage point' outside society to produce 'special insight into the world he stands apart from'. Such a view is a long and deeply held one in a profession that often requires 'special training and self-belief' and can produce, he says, art that is 'done to us, at us and for us, but not *with* us' (2009: 4).

Cameron's polemic against dominant forms of cultural authority is nicely underscored by this description of traditional arts organizations producing work that is done *to* and *for* people. Cameron sees the future viability and vibrancy of the cultural sector as requiring a radical change in the relationships between arts organizations and their publics (2009).

This is not to suggest that there is an unproblematic relationship between engaging audiences on the one hand and political empowerment on the other. Freshwater argues that the belief that participation empowers audiences has become a 'compelling orthodoxy' in theatre and performance studies, an orthodoxy that is often 'reductively and uncritically' applied (2009: 56). She gives the example of the UK theatre critic for the Guardian Lyn Gardner's description of the appetite of contemporary audiences for active engagement and its connection to political empowerment: 'The audiences are already storming the barricades, it is up to the rest of us to give them a helping hand because the revolution has already started without us …' (quoted in Freshwater 2009: 56). For this chapter the argument is not that there is an automatic equation of participation with empowerment or political agency, rather that the Open Stage project, in fostering the active participation of community members, is effectively reviewing and reassessing the assumed cultural authority of arts organizations. Further, just as there is nothing inherently politically radical about audience participation, there is no guarantee that all exercises in audience engagement are of equal artistic quality. However, a number of features testify to the quality of the Open Stage project; it is a long-term commitment to produce not only an artistic product (in the form of a season of work in 2012) but also skill development for participants; it takes a whole of organization approach; and is led by a partnership between community members and TRSE staff. It is clear, too, that the project is likely to meet the need, identified by TRSE's artistic director Kerry Michael, to provoke debate about the role and authority of arts organizations.

Further, Open Stage demonstrates the capacity of cultural organizations to review and reform their responsiveness to the diverse publics and communities they are supposed to serve. In so doing, the outcomes are not about enfranchising the audience as consumer; rather they speak to the empowerment and active participation of communities in shaping institutions in the public sphere, thus underwriting Bauman's call for the strengthening of social cohesion through interaction, dialogue, negotiation and mutual understanding.

Acknowledgements

I am grateful to Kerry Michael and Charlotte Handel from the Theatre Royal Stratford East for their time and for generously sharing their thoughts on the Open Stage project. I would also like to thank John Holden for his comments on this chapter.

Interviews

Handel, C., manager, Open Stage, Theatre Royal Stratford East, interviewed 13 December 2010.
Handel, C. manager, Open Stage, Theatre Royal Stratford East, interviewed 2 May 2011.
Michael, K., artistic director, Theatre Royal Stratford East, interviewed 2 May 2011.

References

Bauman, Z. (2008), *Does Ethics Have a Chance in a World of Consumers?* Cambridge, MA: Harvard University Press.

Boorsma, M. (2006), 'A Strategic Logic for Arts Marketing: Integrating Customer Value and Artistic Objectives', *International Journal of Cultural Policy*, 12:1, pp. 73–92.

Bourdieu, P. (2000), *Distinction: A Social Critique of the Judgement of Taste*, R. Nice (Trans.), Cambridge, MA: Harvard University Press.

Calouste Gulbenkian Foundation (2011), http://www.gulbenkian.pt/index.php?article=3129&langId=2&format=402 (accessed 12 July).

Cameron, B. (2009), *On the Brink of a New Chapter: Arts in the 21st Century*, Australia Council Arts Marketing Summit, http://www.australiacouncil.gov.au/the_arts/features/ben_cameron._on_the_brink_of_a_new chapter_arts_in_the_21st_century (accessed 30 January 2011).

Department of Culture, Media and Sport (DCMS) (2007), *Inspiration, Identity, Learning: The Value of Museums, Second Study*, London: DCMS.

Department for Work and Pensions (DWP) (2011), *Working Together: UK National Action Plan on Social Inclusion*, 2008–2010, http://www.dwp.gov.uk/publications/policy-publications/uk-national-report/uk-national-action-plan (accessed 6 September 2011).

Durrer, V. & Miles, S. (2009), 'New Perspectives on the Role of Cultural Intermediaries in Social Inclusion in the UK', *Consumption, Markets & Culture*, 12: 3, pp. 225–241.

Eyre, R. & Wright, N. (2000), *Changing Stages*, London: Bloomsbury.

Freshwater, H. (2009), *Theatre and Audience*, Basingstoke, Hampshire: Palgrave Macmillan.

Gardiner, L. (2011), 'The Passion – Review', *The Guardian*, 24 April, http://www.guardian.co.uk (accessed 11 July 2011).

Handel, C. (2010), *Stratford East Open Stage Report*, Theatre Royal Stratford East.

Kurin, R. (1997), *Reflections of a Cultural Broker: A View from the Smithsonian*, Washington, Smithsonian Institution Press.

Leadbeater, C. (2009), *The Art of With*, Cornerhouse Manchester, Creative Commons UK, http://www.cornerhouse.org/wp-content/uploads/old_site/media/Learn/The%20Art%20of%20With.pdf. (accessed August 2011).

National Theatre of Wales (2011), http://nationaltheatrewales.org/about#a#learningandparticipation (accessed 11 July 2011).

Negus, K. (2002), 'The Work of Cultural Intermediaries and the Enduring Distance between Production and Consumption', *Cultural Studies*, 16: 4, pp. 501–515.

Open Stage (2011), Theatre Royal Stratford East, http://www.openstage2012.com/?category_name=open-stage (accessed 10 July 2011).

Ross, M. (2004), 'Interpreting the New Museology', *Museum and Society*, 2: 2, pp. 84–103.

Tait, S. (2011), 'Presenting the World's Biggest Art Prize: the £175,000 Gulbenkian', *The Independent*, 8 May, http://www.independent.co.uk/arts-entertainment/art/news/presenting-the-worlds-biggest-art-prize-the-163175000-gulbenkian-2280813.html. (accessed 12 July 2011).

Theatre Royal Stratford East (2008), *Annual Report*, January to December.

——— (2010), *Annual Report*, Jan 2009–March 2010.

Chapter 4

All the World's a Stage: Venues and Settings, and Their Role in Shaping Patterns of Arts Participation

Alan Brown

Theatres are the best way to keep people from the arts.

(Simon Dove, Utrecht Festival, Dance/USA Forum, January 2011)

All arts activities occur in the context of a physical or virtual setting, whether an automobile, a concert hall or Facebook.[1] Different settings have different economic, social, behavioural and symbolic connotations (Conner 2008). Consider, for example, the differences between seeing a great work of art in a museum versus seeing a reproduction of the same work of art on the kitchen wall every day for ten or twenty years. Surely both experiences create meaning for the viewer, although the settings hold radically different value and legitimacy to society.

Why will some people engage with art in one setting, but not another? For example, why will someone watch great drama on television at home, but never darken the door of a theatre? Why will someone listen to classical music in a place of worship, but not a concert hall?

This chapter explores the role that setting plays in arts experiences, and challenges artists and arts organizations to think more broadly and more creatively about *where* audiences encounter art. The term 'setting' refers to the many spaces, venues and locations where arts experiences take place, and is used intentionally to broaden the discussion beyond conventional arts facilities. Settings may be formal or informal, temporary or permanent, public or private, and physical or virtual. In the broadest sense, 'setting' is a sort of meeting ground between artist and audience – a place both parties occupy for a finite period of time to exchange ideas and create meaning.

Two underlying hypotheses compel this chapter. The first is that setting plays an increasingly important role as a decision factor among cultural consumers, and therefore is a subtle, if not profound, driver of arts participation. The second is based on a wealth of anecdotal evidence: artists and arts organizations are choosing to create and present art in a wider range of settings that both animate the art and capture the imagination of audiences in new ways.

The need to more fully understand the inter-relationships between setting and art is long overdue. With some notable exceptions,[2] the arts sector lacks a strong body of critical thinking about the changing nature of venues and settings for contemporary arts experiences and, specifically, how different settings amplify or detract from participation. Yet outside the arts, a wealth of related literature delves into placemaking, the psychology of architecture, and the role of public art in civic identity (see, e.g., Green 2011). Much of this work suggests that setting plays a much larger and more significant role than that of an empty vessel for artistic activity. Theatres, concert halls and museums are conducive to certain kinds of exchange between art and people. But meaningful exchange occurs with greater frequency in many other settings, from old breweries to planetariums, abandoned subway platforms, barges, cinemas and community bookstores. With the proliferation of virtual spaces for arts programmes, it seems now that all the world's a stage.

The problem with fixed arts facilities

Historically, venues and the art that appears in them have enjoyed a close relationship: sacred music composed specifically for reverberant cathedrals, Viennese opera houses, Parisian cabarets and the American jazz clubs of the 1930s all had unique and idiosyncratic connections to their respective art forms. In his 2010 TED talk, 'The True Power of the Performing Arts', Ben Cameron, programme director for the arts at the Doris Duke Charitable Foundation, acknowledged that many purpose-built arts venues 'were designed to ossify the ideal relationship between artist and audience most appropriate for the 19th century' (Cameron 2010). This sentiment is echoed by Duncan Webb, a leading arts facility consultant, who argues that arts facilities have not evolved or adapted to the changing expectations and needs of contemporary artists, audiences and communities.

The larger problem with the infrastructure of arts facilities is that it is fixed and slow to change, while culture is changing more and more rapidly. Even as new performing arts centres open in places like Kansas City and Las Vegas, industry leaders are talking about the need to adapt and repurpose these types of facilities to accommodate programmes that serve a larger public (Bruner Loeb 2010). Purpose-built theatres lag behind current-day cultural norms by many years. The problem is exacerbated when new facilities are modeled on old ones, perpetuating derivative thinking by architects, theatre consultants and their clients who seldom take the time to consider what experiences future generations of artists and audiences will require.

Arts spaces have become increasingly flexible and diverse over the past fifty years. The proliferation of multi-purpose theatres, high school auditoriums and performing arts centres in the second half of the twentieth century began to deconstruct important historical relationships. Over the years, audiences in many cities and towns have grown accustomed to using the same venue for a wide array of live events, from poetry slams to chamber music concerts. While multi-purpose venues can expand access to the arts, important connections between art and setting have been lost.

Continued diversification and growth in population will inevitably lead to a shift in policy towards 'democratizing culture' and a re-allocation of resources to organizations, programmes and venues outside of the major cultural centres.[3] Research indicates that in the United States, white Americans use purpose-built arts facilities at several times the rate that Hispanics and African Americans use them. In contrast, populations of colour report using places of worship and informal settings at several times the rate of whites (Brown 2008). It is difficult to know the extent to which negative attitudes and perceptions about arts venues are a barrier as opposed to other factors such as location, cost or lack of culturally relevant programming.

Inviting audiences to spaces they do not want to visit is a losing proposition, especially when they *do* show up and feel out of place. Without a clearer perspective on the dynamics between audience, artist and setting, the arts sector will not develop the capacity it needs to engage the next generation of art lovers.

Symbolic identification and behaviour change

Consumers have deep-seated feelings about arts spaces, describing them as 'friendly', 'welcoming', or 'cold', or 'intimidating' – attributes often ascribed to people. For those who have never visited a facility, these feelings may relate to location and perceptions of safety and parking availability. For those with past experiences, feelings about a facility can be influenced by factors such as seat comfort, acoustics and the way they have been treated by ushers and ticket sellers. Memories of past experiences in certain venues and settings, as well as their historical significance and meaning to the community, shape expectations for what is appropriate and possible in those spaces.

Venues also take on symbolic meanings, either based on actual experience or transmitted through social networks. Some young people reject theatres and concert halls as settings for their parents' and grandparents' generations. Others feel that formal arts venues impose stifling social norms or elicit what Bourdieu described in his research on museum visitors as 'a profound feeling of unworthiness and incompetence' (Bourdieu 1991).

The architecture and design of arts venues also influence the behaviours that occur within them. Winifred Gallagher asserts that 'people feel best in settings that, like parks and cars, foster a sense of control, impose few constraints, and offer multiple choices' (1999: 74). Studies in the fields of architecture and environmental psychology point to the profound role that environment plays in driving behaviour. Speaking at the American Institute of Architects annual convention, Fred Gage, the Salk Institute neuroscientist, explained:

> As neuroscientists, we believe that the brain is the organ that controls behavior, that genes control the blueprint, the design, and the structure of the brain, but the environment can modulate the function of genes, and our behaviour. Architectural design changes our brain and our behaviour.
>
> (as quoted in Zeisel 2006)

Just as certain sounds and scents evoke memories, setting plays a key role in stimulating and reinforcing human behaviour. Psychologists identify setting as a trigger for both constructive and destructive behaviours. Moving someone into a new setting re-contextualizes the behaviour in question and resets the relationship between space and behaviour. Old sights, smells and symbolic cues are no longer present, thus removing a barrier to the desired behaviour.

Re-contextualizing art in a different setting, therefore, is a form of stimulus control that can trigger new behaviour (i.e., attendance) and free the art from negative associations and other barriers. When the Boston Lyric Opera offered two free outdoor performances of *Carmen* in the Boston Common, roughly 120,000 people showed up, according to official estimates – nearly two-thirds of whom were under the age of 35, and 30 per cent at their very first opera.[4] More recently, the San Francisco Opera attracted over 30,000 people to its September 2011 live digital broadcast of Puccini's *Turandot* at AT&T ballpark. The phenomenal success of la Folle Journée, France's largest classical music festival, may be ascribed in large part to creative uses of setting and alternative formats (for instance, no concert lasts more than 45 minutes).[5]

It seems that younger adults attach different values to both setting and format than their older counterparts. Arts groups' efforts to attract younger audiences, even when initially successful, are sometimes thwarted by the actual experience that young people have when they show up and do not see their peer group in attendance. When the setting is changed, however, the positive experience of younger audiences can be reinforced, such as when the London Sinfonietta performed Steve Reich's music in the Oskar Schindler factory in Krakow, Poland (Bujic 2009). Other variables, such as curtain time, can also be adjusted to attract different audiences, such as Paul Winter's popular solstice celebrations at New York City's

Figure 4.1: The 2009 Sacrum Profanum Festival in Krakow, Poland, included performances in the Museum of Urban Engineering, located in an old tram terminus and depot station. (Photo: Pawel Suder).

Cathedral of St. John the Divine, which begin at 4:30 a.m. In altering setting and format, artists and curators can invoke cultural norms not typically associated with arts attendance and begin to address some of the underlying barriers to attendance.

Audience sovereignty

Consumers increasingly expect a high degree of interactivity and engagement in their leisure pursuits, from gaming to reality TV and theme parks. Everywhere one looks, consumers are being offered choices that were not previously available. Instead of buying a doll, a young girl can go online and design her own. The crowdsourcing ethos is a manifestation of this shift, along with the pervasive assumption that consumers are entitled to provide feedback on every product, service or webpage they use.

There is much talk in the arts sector about allowing audiences and visitors to 'co-author' meaning, but still a good deal of scepticism about what this really means, and how to do it. Lynne Conner uses the term 'sovereignty' to characterize the authority that audiences want over their arts experiences (2008: 6). At a focus group discussion several years ago, young adults were asked to narrate an 'imaginary tour' of a hypothetical jazz venue. With the aid of a glass of wine, they designed the next generation of concert facilities defined largely around choice-making. During the day, the venue would be open as a coffee house/music lounge, where anyone can come to hear, share and acquire music. At night, it would transition to a venue for live concerts where patrons can move fluidly between different spaces designed for intensive listening, 'partial-attention' listening, and socializing while watching the concert on a large screen.

Static experiences of all sorts will grow increasingly problematic, especially those that do not offer audience members any choices to make, such as when to get up, when to get a drink, when to talk – all of which are available in the theatre of the home. The need to offer consumers more opportunities to personalize their experiences has implications for both the art itself, in terms of a diminishing audience for what some consider 'passive' experiences, and most likely foreshadows waning interest in the more restrictive settings in which professionalized art is offered. In the realm of participatory arts, recent studies have uncovered a rich tapestry of activity in a wide range of informal and non-traditional community settings such as coffee houses, neighbourhood art centres, commercial stores and parks (see Alvarez 2005; and Wali et al. 2002). Perhaps this high level of accessibility is one reason why participation in arts creation has not declined as much as attendance-based participation (Novak-Leonard & Brown 2008).

Settings and socialization

In his seminal text *Art as Experience*, John Dewey wrote that music, dance, drama, painting and sculpture and the buildings that housed them served an inherently social purpose over the centuries (Dewey 2005). Eating, drinking, socializing, flirting and more serious discourse were always central to arts experiences. Only in the last few hundred years have the arts been restricted to 'sacred place[s] where there is no touching and no talking' (Conner 2008). Settings for arts programmes are distinguished by the types of social interactions that they permit both inside and outside of the audience chamber or gallery spaces. What does it signal to arriving audience members, for example, when they see other patrons sitting in intimate seating areas socializing before a concert – or lingering afterwards?

Settings are important because, for a finite period of time, they create 'community'. But, what kind of 'community' do they really create, and for whom? Sociologist Elijah Anderson suggests that public spaces can serve as 'cosmopolitan canopies' where people from different walks of life converge (Anderson 2004). Under these 'canopies', race, class, and other conventions of social hierarchy matter less. Everyone has an opportunity to 'belong'. Not everyone, of course, wants to be under Anderson's umbrella, but the concept is useful because it suggests that arts facilities can serve not only as meeting places for like-minded art lovers, but as canopies for our increasingly diverse communities.

Creating 'community' is not dependent on interpersonal contact alone, since most people who visit arts facilities speak directly with only a few other people. The larger meaning of 'community' relates more to what French sociologist Émile Durkheim described as the 'collective effervescence' – when the 'act of congregating' becomes a 'powerful stimulant' – and the outcome cannot be predicted by individual responses alone (Durkheim 1995).

Subtle design features can have a profound impact. What is the effect on theatregoers, for example, when they can see the faces of other audience members during a performance, as opposed to when they can only see the backs of heads? As humans, we instinctually mimic one another, thereby negotiating meaning and constructing bonds that sustain and protect us (Hatfield 1994). It is difficult to absorb the emotional reactions of other audience members in a totally darkened auditorium, except by hearing them. Seating configurations that allow for more visual interaction among audience members, aided by sufficient lighting, can positively affect the audience experience.

The need to offer more sociable, intimate, informal and comfortable environments for arts programmes has become an urgent priority, according to Diane Paulus, the visionary artistic director of American Repertory Theatre in Cambridge, Massachusetts, who refers to herself as 'a crusader for expanding the ways and the places where people can come to the theatre'.[6] The higher premium attached to the social aspect of arts attendance can be seen in facility projects ranging from Arena Stage's $130 million transformation (devoted to improving the audience experience *outside* of its theatres, in large part) to New York's Le Poisson Rouge, a hybrid social/performance space 'serving art and alcohol' – undoubtedly one of the most talked-about facilities in recent memory.

As audiences become more assertive about shaping their own cultural experiences, it is little wonder they are turning to a broader array of venues and settings. Consumers who reject one setting in favor of another are merely enacting a form of sovereignty they are regularly given, and have come to expect, from other entertainment experiences.

Settings for digitized art

The proliferation of settings extends to virtual spaces and physical spaces designed for the enjoyment of digital content. Once digitized, art can be experienced anywhere – on a computer screen at work, on a mobile device at the gym or on a large screen in a movie theatre. Digitized art is also largely a sunk cost; the incremental expense of showing it again is a fraction of the cost of its original production.

In 2011, for the first time, the Metropolitan Opera turned a profit on its live high-definition broadcasts into movie theatres. Over two million people watch these broadcasts worldwide every year. The Met's cinema patrons enjoy a good social dynamic (they applaud together and mingle) and often comment about the excellent visual experience: 'The close-ups were so tight you could see a tear slowly trickling down the tenor's face', and 'the soprano's fingernail polish didn't match the color on her toes, though she did nail the high C' (Associated Press 2010). Other arts groups such as the National Theatre of Great Britain and the Los Angeles Philharmonic have also entered the digital marketplace with high quality programmes. The movie theatre is now a valued setting for arts programmes. This is significant because movie theatres – one of the dominant settings for entertainment outside of the home – are accessible to nearly everyone. With their reclining seats, cup holders, and individual arm rests, movie theatres set the standard by which other venues are judged. Have you been to a luxury cinema lately?

In twenty or thirty years, it is quite possible that millions of people around the globe will be going to movie theatres to watch high quality digital broadcasts of the best opera, dance, classical music, stage plays and musicals in the world, for a fraction of the price of a ticket to a live performance. From a policy standpoint, this would be a fantastic outcome in terms of increasing public participation in the arts, particularly for residents of rural areas where live programmes are not available at all. Will theatres and concert halls grow darker and darker as consumers drive instead to their local multiplex to see first-class international productions?

Digital experiences, as they gain in quality and selection, will be seen as an inexpensive and attractive alternative to live performance, especially when the setting affords more social benefits and creature comforts than are available in theatres and concert halls. Arts groups have a limited window of time to integrate digital content into their programmes and facilities, or they will forego significant opportunities to develop new audiences and regenerate interest in their art forms.

The role of arts facilities in placemaking

A new focus on the arts' role in urban revitalization, neighbourhood development and civic dialogue speaks to a shift in priority from art as a disembodied commodity for those who can afford it, to art as a fully integrated element of community life (Markusen & Gadwa 2010).

Two well-funded examples are the ArtPlace grant initiative,[7] supported by a consortium of foundations, and the National Endowment for the Arts' Our Town Initiative,[8] both designed to support a variety of projects that integrate art with civic priorities such as livability and neighbourhood renewal. This signals a new chapter in the central narrative of the public value of the arts. More often, investments in art must generate not only 'excellent' art but also art that connects people with their communities in tangible, practical ways – a ratcheting-up of desired outcomes borne out of a desire to gain a more central role for the arts in civic life. This impulse amongst funders is supported by a growing body of research linking arts and cultural assets with neighbourhood vitality (See Nowak 2007; and Stern & Seifert 2008).

An implication of this repositioning is the pressure it exerts on cultural facilities to play a more integral and intentional role in civic life. The decades-old value system underlying centrally located stand-alone cultural facilities that are disconnected from the urban fabric is giving way to an ethos that supports more decentralized networks of smaller, re-purposed and re-used facilities that have more intimate and immediate relationships with their surroundings.

Cultural policy rarely addresses the question of what communities need from their cultural facilities with much clarity. A few cultural planning processes, such as the one completed by the City of San Jose in 2010, focus on the need to support small-scale venues scattered throughout a community, 'both downtown and in neighbourhood business districts' (Plettner & Saunders 2011). A new breed of spaces for arts-based creative exchange has emerged, such as the Hyde Park Art Center in Chicago and Taller Puertorriqueño in Philadelphia, often combining libraries, exhibition spaces, performance spaces, classrooms, media labs, retail spaces, cafés and technology-rich meeting spaces.

Between 2005 and 2008, a consortium of public agencies in Canada sought to better understand the existing cultural infrastructure in order to anticipate future needs.[9] Scholars articulated a need for four types of arts, cultural and creative spaces:

1. Multi-use hubs that bring together arts, culture, heritage and library facilities;
2. Incubator spaces that support creative exchange between and among artists, entrepreneurs and the public;
3. Multi-sector 'convergence spaces' that foster networking and 'random collision' between creative workers; and
4. Long-term artist live/work spaces.

(Duxbury 2008)

Arts and cultural facilities must play a far more central role in the intellectual, creative, social and entrepreneurial lives of their communities than they do now. It is also clear that community needs will be increasingly satisfied by temporary, movable, and low-cost 'semi-permanent' venues that can respond more flexibly to a community's unique and changing needs. This can be seen in the growing number of 'pop-up' arts programmes and facilities around the world, ranging from Chicago's Pop-Up Art Loop™ project[10] and the Chanel Mobile Art Pavilion[11] to the expanding realm of 'urban ephemera' – parades, festivals and other short-lived or spontaneous events that transform urban areas and inject an element of surprise into life's routines.[12]

When the siting and design of arts facilities reflect their communities and mesh with their surroundings in novel ways, the results can foster community engagement in the arts and add immeasurably to a community's sense of place. Consider, for example, the Mart Theatre[13] in Skipton, a small agricultural town in the Yorkshire region of the United Kingdom, where city planners identified an underutilized livestock market as a site for live performing arts programmes. The Mart Theatre opened in 2005 with an 'artistic programme designed to address local cultural and economic needs', including weekend art fairs ('Art in the Pen') and theatrical productions on weekend nights exploring, among other things, intersections between art and agriculture.

Artists as curators of setting

While some artists prefer to perform and exhibit in prestigious venues with first-class technical capacities, good acoustics and comfortable dressing rooms, others, such as choreographers Elizabeth Streb and Emily Johnson, are decidedly moving beyond conventional spaces and asserting a license to design the settings in which their art is experienced, as well as the art itself. Streb's Lab for Action Mechanics (or S.L.A.M.) in Brooklyn's Williamsburg neighbourhood was designed specifically to allow and encourage audience members to play an active role in their experiences, and embodies Streb's desire to embed her work in a community context. Minneapolis-based Emily Johnson's work blurs many lines, including the lines between artist, audience and setting. Her pieces often take the form of installations that engage audiences in architectural spaces and environments – such as vacant office spaces and IMAX theatres – that are part and parcel of her artistic impulse.

Many artists draw inspiration from the setting itself, either making thematic connections or incorporating physical elements of the space into their artistic concepts. One of the more imaginative examples in recent memory was Gotham Chamber Orchestra's 2010 production of *Il Mondo Della Luna/The World in the Moon*, an obscure Haydn opera staged in the Hayden Planetarium of the American Museum of Natural History in New York, under the direction of Diane Paulus.[14] Another notable example of the blending of setting and art is *Sleep No More*, a roving theatrical production by Punchdrunk, the British immersive theatre troupe, in which 'Lines between space, performer and spectator are constantly shifting'.[15] Billed as an 'indoor promenade performance' at a converted warehouse space in New York City, audience members wander around the venue charting their own course and encountering scenes along the way.

A growing number of arts groups, such as Woodshed Collective (New York) and Da Camera Society (Los Angeles), are building identities around the unique settings in

Figure 4.2: The 2010 Gotham Chamber Orchestra production of *Il Mondo della Luna* at the Hayden Planetarium. (Photo: Judith Levitt for The New York Times).

which their work is experienced. While site-specific work is nothing new, artists seem to be demanding more control over the settings in which their work is experienced. This can be understood both in economic terms – as a means of accessing more affordable spaces, and on artistic terms – as a means of bypassing cultural gatekeepers and gaining more creative control over the entirety of the arts experience, if only to relinquish it back to the audience.

Creating more intimate and direct connections with audiences is an over-riding need for talented but discontented young artists like violist Charith Premawardhana, founder of Classical Revolution,[16] a musician-driven performance network. Frustrated with the system of agents, unions, venues, and institutions that stand between art and people, Premawardhana seeks to reclaim the act of music-making. 'It's *our* experience to enjoy the way *we* want to,' he explains. 'I think younger musicians have a different attitude. We need to make our own work happen on our own terms.'

Increasing numbers of visual artists, musicians, choreographers, and theatre and opera directors are creating and adapting work for settings that add an important element to the artistic experience. This presents a challenge to curators and artistic planners who must think anew about existing and alternative spaces that will accommodate the work

Figure 4.3: A Classical Revolution concert at the Revolution café in San Francisco. (Photo: Henry Story).

of ambitous, untethered artists whose work aims to explore the combustion of art and setting.

As Howard Becker noted in his 2004 essay 'Jazz Places', artists' work is shaped by the many settings in which they work (Becker 2004). It is essential, therefore, to think of setting not only as a variable in the audience experience but also as a critical aspect of the aesthetic development of artists.

Conclusion

Settings are imbued with meaning, much as art has different meanings to different people. In the economy of meaning, setting is a currency, just as art is a currency (Sharpe 2011). As consumers grow increasingly efficient at editing, organizing and remixing the art in their lives, so too are they increasingly comfortable curating the settings where they interact with art. In doing so, they form likes and dislikes for certain settings, which, in turn, reshapes patterns of arts participation.

All of this suggests a need for modern-day curators and artistic directors to canvass their communities for indigenous settings for art, much like an archaeologist scours the earth for clues to human history. Where, amid the architectural detritus of a once-bustling Midwestern town, might jazz take on a new life? Where along the streetscape can visual art find a new audience? Where are the unexpected stages in your community, waiting to be animated?

Many artists and arts groups prefer not to perform or exhibit in unconventional settings. There are financial obstacles, artistic limitations, technical barriers and a host of other legitimate reasons for keeping art in purpose-built venues. Nonetheless, the fact remains that setting and format are under-leveraged variables in the stubborn calculus of audience development.

Correcting this situation will require a paradigm shift in the way that art is curated. Effective artistic leaders will need to know their communities as well as their art forms, and will need to take artistic cues not only from art and artists, but from settings and formats, as well. An orchestra, for example, might identify a space of historic significance to its community, and then curate a musical programme particularly suited for that space, and for the audience that will be drawn to it.

Adapting old spaces and using found spaces are two approaches to re-contextualizing art, but a third approach is necessary. Fresh thinking is needed to design an entirely new breed of arts venues that blend together social, artistic and creative possibilities, both live and digital. The New World Center in Miami Beach is a laboratory for exploring new presentation formats and represents a significant step forward in the re-thinking of arts venues. But a great deal more experimentation is needed. Until and unless we can break the chain of derivative thinking about how arts spaces should be designed, the infrastructure will grow obsolete on an ever-shortening timeline.

The public has already asserted sovereignty over where it engages with art. Now the arts sector must apply its creative energies to discovering the settings where art will resonate with different communities, especially those without museums and theatres. In order to gain the higher levels of public support and funding that they seek, arts groups will need to find and use settings that re-contextualize art and make their programmes relevant to a broader public.

Setting is a critical backdrop to arts participation. In a marketplace haunted by uncertainty, setting is one of the few variables that artists and curators can, and must, use imaginatively.

The time has come to reconsider the trade-offs of presenting art in a broader range of settings that engage communities in new and exciting ways. As our forbears discovered centuries ago, the marriage of art and setting can be divine.

Acknowledgements

This chapter would not have been possible without the great work of other researchers, writers, consultants and practitioners, including Ben Cameron, Melissa Chan, Lynne Conner, Betty Farrell, Arlene Goldbard, Nick Herd, John Holden, Nan Keeton, Peter Linett, Josephine Ramirez, Diane Ragsdale, Duncan Webb and Steven Wolff. Charith Premawardhana, founder of Classical Revolution, was especially generous in sharing his passion for a new approach to concertizing. Finally, I am especially indebted to Kyle Marinshaw of WolfBrown for his detailed research and assistance in outlining the chapter.

References

Anderson, E. (2004), 'The Cosmopolitan Canopy', *Annals of the American Academy of Political and Social Science*, 595: 1 (September), pp. 14–31.

Associated Press (2010), *Met Opera Adds 300 Theatres for HD Broadcasts*, Crain's New York Business.om, September 1, http://www.crainsnewyork.com/article/20100901/FREE/100909978 (accessed 18 March 2012).

Becker, H. (2004), 'Jazz Places', in A. Bennett & R. Peterson (eds), *Music Scenes: Local, Translocal, and Virtual*, Nashville Tennessee: Vanderbilt University Press, pp. 17–27, http://home.earthlink.net/~hsbecker/articles/places.html (accessed 18 March 2012).

Bourdieu, P. (1991), *The Love of Art: European Art Museums and Their Public*, Stanford: Stanford University Press.

Brown, A. & Daniel, T. (2008), *The Arts Activities of Dallas Independent School District Students*, Research Commissioned by Big Thought, Dallas Arts Learning Initiative, WolfBrown, http://www.bigthought.org/LinkClick.aspx?fileticket=U8F6pyt9Weg%3D (accessed 18 March 2012).

Brown, A., Novak, J. & Kitchener, A. (2008), *Cultural Engagement in California's Inland Regions*, WolfBrown, http://irvine.org/publications/publications-by-topic/arts (accessed 18 March 2012).

Bruner Loeb forum (2010), *City as a Stage: Placemaking for the Performing Arts*, Performing Arts Center of Los Angeles County, http://www.brunerloeb.org/images/fora/LA Program 2010.pdf. (accessed 18 March 2012).

Bujic, H. (2009), 'New Ears', *Arts Professional*, 205 (November 2), p. 11.

Cameron, B. (2010), 'The True Power of the Performing Arts', *TEDxYYC*, recorded February, http://www.ted.com/talks/ben_cameron_tedxyyc.html (accessed 18 March 2012).

Conner, L. (2008), 'In and Out of the Dark, A Theory of Audience Behaviour from Sophocles to Spoken Word', in W. Ivey & S. Tepper (eds), *Engaging Art: The Next Great Transformation of America's Cultural Life*, London: Routledge Press.

Dewey, J. (2005), *Art as Experience* (first published 1934), Perigee Books.

Durkheim, É. (1995), *The Elementary Forms of the Religious Life* (1912, English translation by Joseph Swain: 1915), New York: Free Press.

Duxbury, N. (ed.) (2008), *Under Construction: The State of Cultural Infrastructure in Canada*, The Centre of Expertise on Culture and Communities, Burnaby, CA: Simon Fraser University.

Goldbard, A. (2006), *New Creative Community: The Art of Cultural Development*, Oakland, CA, New Village Press, http://arlenegoldbard.com/books/newcc/ (accessed 18 March 2012).

Green, A. (2011), 'Reading about Public Art', Axisweb, http://www.axisweb.org/dlFull.aspx?ESSAYID=56 (accessed 14 December 2011).

Hatfield, E., Cacioppo, J.T. & Rapson, R. L. (1994), *Emotional Contagion*, Cambridge: Cambridge University Press.

Lancaster, H., Kyte, S., Craik, J. & Schippers, H. (2010), *Redefining Places for Art: Exploring the Dynamics of Performance and Location*, St. Lucia, Queensland: Griffith University.

Markusen, A. & Gadwa, A. (2010), 'Creative Placemaking', *The Mayors' Institute on City Design*, the National Endowment for the Arts in partnership with the United States Conference of Mayors and American Architectural Foundation, http://arts.gov/pub/pubDesign.php. (accessed 18 March 2012).

Novak-Leonard, J. & Brown, A. (2008), *Beyond Attendance: A Multi-Modal Understanding of Arts Participation*, National Endowment for the Arts' Survey of Public Participation in the Arts, WolfBrown.

Nowak, J. (2007), *Creativity and Neighborhood Development: Strategies for Community Investment*, Philadelphia: TRFund.

Plettner, D. & Saunders, V. (2011), *Cultural Connection: San Jose's Cultural Plan for 2011–2020*, City of San Jose Office of Cultural Affairs, overview at http://www.sanjoseculture.org/printable.php?pid=99210 (accessed 18 March 2012).

Prochaska, J.O. & DiClemente, C.C. (1986), 'Toward a Comprehensive Model of Change', in W.R. Miller & N. Heather (eds), *Treating Addictive Behaviors: Processes of Change*, Plenum Press.

Ragsdale, D. (2010), 'The Excellence Barrier', keynote address prepared for the Washington State Arts Council, available at http://www.artsjournal.com/jumper/wp-content/uploads/2010/09/Ragsdale-The-Excellence-Barrier-WSAA-2010.pdf. (accessed 18 March 2012).

Sharpe, B. (2011), *Economies of Life: Patterns of Health and Wealth*, UK, Triarchy Press, www.triarchypress.com/pages/economies_of_life.htm. (accessed 18 March 2012).

Stern, M. & Seifert, S. (2008), 'From Creative Economy to Creative Society', *Creativity & Change*, a collaboration of the Social Impact of the Arts Project and The Reinvestment Fund, overview at http://www.trfund.com/resource/creativity.html.

Wali, A., Severson, R. & Longoni, M. (2002), 'Informal Arts: Finding Cohesion, Capacity and Other Cultural Benefits in Unexpected Places', *GIA Reader*, 13:3, http://www2.colum.edu/center_for_arts_policy/community_informal_arts.htm. (accessed 18 March 2012).

WolfBrown (2011), *Jazz Audience Initiative*, commissioned by Jazz Arts Group of Columbus, Ohio, with funding support from the Doris Duke Charitable Foundation, http://wolfbrown.com/index.php?page=jazz-audiences-initiative (accessed 18 March 2012).

Zeisel, J. (2006), *Inquiry by Design: Environment/Behavior/Neuroscience in Architecture, Interiors, Landscape, and Planning*, New York: Norton.

Notes

1   For example, StreamJam, a software application developed by The Electric Sheep Company, allows users to 'attend' live concerts within the Facebook environment. 'When the full version of StreamJam is launched, it will be a perpetual 24/7 online music festival with venues embedded on pages across the Web.' See http://www.electricsheepcompany.com/streamjam/.

2   One publication in particular was especially influential in guiding my thoughts about setting: *Redefining Places for Art: Exploring the dynamics of performance and location* by Helen Lancaster, Suzanne Kyte, Jennifer Craik & Huib Schippers, Queensland Conservatorium Research Centre, Griffith University (2010). Melissa M. Chan, a graduate of Columbia University, also made a fine contribution to this topic with her masters thesis paper, 'Second Chances: Exploring the role of unexpected context in live performance to rekindle classical music's relationship with today's audience', 2010 (unpublished).

3   Achieving more equitable access to culture was a theme of the Future of the City symposium in June 2011, organized by the University of Chicago. See http://futureofthecity.uchicago.edu/arts/.

4   These figures derive from a survey of 762 *Carmen on the Common* attenders; research conducted for the Boston Lyric Opera by Audience Insight LLC of Fairfield, Connecticut, 2002.

5   La Folle Journée is a French annual classical music festival held in Nantes. According to the organization's website, 'la Folle Journée offers a new perspective on concerts that attracts and instructs new audiences of all ages by doing away with the unchanging and rather predictable rituals of conventional concerts.' For more information, see http://www.follejournee.fr/index.php?option=com_content&view=article&id=47&Itemid=85&lang=en. Other cities have developed their own festivals based on the format of La Folle Journée, including Madrid, Bilbao, Tokyo, Rio de Janeiro and Warsaw.

6   The creation of inviting social environments to attract younger audiences was a recurrent theme at a 2010 symposium on the twenty-first century arts center, hosted by Dartmouth College. The entire proceedings were videotaped and are posted in time-marked segments at http://hop.dartmouth.edu/uncategorised/arts-of-the-21st-century.

7   'ArtPlace believes that art, culture and creativity expressed powerfully through place can create vibrant communities, thus increasing the desire and the economic opportunity for people to thrive in place. It is all about the local.' – from www.artplaceamerica.org.

8   See http://www.nea.gov/national/ourtown/index.php.

9   The Centre of Expertise on Culture and Communities (CECC), administered at Simon Fraser University from 2005 to 2008, was an extensive research project into cultural infrastructure in Canada. For a list of publications, see http://www.cultureandcommunities.ca/resources_infrastructure.html.

10 See http://www.popupartloop.com/index.php.

11 The Chanel Mobile Art Pavilion was a traveling exhibit created by Karl Lagerfeld and Zaha Hadid. For a video tour of the inflatable venue, see http://www.chanel-mobileart.com/. The architecture field has long been fascinated with temporary, inflatable and mobile structures: http://weburbanist.com/2011/09/09/blow-up-buildings-17-inflatable-works-of-mobile-architecture/.

12 Examples of urban ephemera include The Big Dance, a large scale event planned in conjunction with the 2012 Olympics in London (see http://www.bigdance2012.com), and The Sultan's Elephant, a show created by the Royal de Luxe theatre company and performed in London in 2006, involving a huge moving mechanical elephant, a giant marionette of a girl and other associated public art installations (see http://www.thesultanselephant.com/about/royaldeluxe.php).

13 See http://www.themarttheatre.org.uk/.

14 For an accounting of the conception of the production in this unusual space, read Matthew Gurewitsch's 14 January 2010 *New York Times* story on the production at www.nytimes.com/2010/01/17/arts/music/17mondo.html?pagewanted=all.

15 See http://sleepnomorenyc.com/, accessed 26 November 2011. Also see Ben Brantley's *New York Times'* review at http://theater.nytimes.com/2011/04/14/theater/reviews/sleep-nomore-is-a-macbeth-in-a-hotel-review.html?ref=theater.

16 Classical Revolution is a musician-driven, zero-budget, multi-city movement to bring chamber music to a wider audience by 'offering performances in highly accessible venues such as bars and cafes, and collaborating with local musicians and artists from various styles and backgrounds. As of early 2012, there were 20 chapters in communities ranging from Portland to Ann Arbor. Marketing is done almost exclusively through Facebook. For more information, see http://www.classicalrevolution.org/.

Chapter 5

In the Context of Their Lives: How Audience Members Make Sense of Performing Arts Experiences

Lois Foreman-Wernet and Brenda Dervin

O ver the last several decades there have been significant shifts in thinking about the arts and their role in our lives.[1] For a variety of social and economic reasons, arts organizations have encountered increased pressure to justify their existence and argue for support from government entities and private funding sources as well as from individual citizens who might take part in the arts. This has resulted in a broadening of how we think about the arts and the gathering of data that help us better understand the impacts of the arts at both the societal and personal levels.

One trend in this regard has been to position the arts as addressing a broad range of societal concerns that contribute to public value or the public good, including such things as fostering community, contributing to economic prosperity, cultivating democracy and enhancing quality of life (see Stevenson et al. 2010; Rumbold 2008; and Wyszomirski 2000). In keeping with this broader understanding of the role of the arts, conceptions both of the arts field and also the idea of arts participation have been greatly enlarged. On one hand, the twentieth-century understanding of 'the arts' as non-profit visual and performing arts has merged into the largely economic-based 'cultural industry' or 'creative sector' (see Balfe & Peters 2000; Chartrand 2000; Cherbo 1998; and Ivey 2008). On the other hand, arts participation has expanded from merely attendance at arts events to include a wide range of cultural practices (see Balfe 2003; Jackson & Herranz 2002; Mulcahy 2006; and Wali & Ostergaard 2010).

A second trend in arts policy and research has been a response to calls for the need to focus on arts experiences from the perspective of the individual (see Belfiore & Bennett 2007; Cheney 2010; and McCarthy et al. 2004). This move recognizes the need to go beyond the use of traditional demographically oriented social science surveys that assess attitudes or participation, to a deeper understanding of how audience members actually experience the arts. In recent years numerous studies have emerged that identify the impacts of arts experiences from the perspective of the individual audience members involved (see Brown 2004; Brown & Novak 2007; DeNora 2000; Radbourne et al. 2010; Radbourne et al. 2009; Pitts & Spencer 2008; and White & Hede 2008).

This chapter contributes to this ongoing line of research through discussion of one methodology that can be used to gather relevant audience data, a summary of general findings of our research using this methodology, and a brief case study from our research that shows how individuals interpret their performing arts experiences within the context of their lives. We assume a fundamental communication framework both as the substance of arts experience and as the appropriate methodology for accessing that experience (Foreman-Wernet & Dervin 2010).

Methodology

The research approach in this chapter aligns with our ongoing twelve-year-old project focusing on everyday sense-making of the arts (Foreman-Wernet & Dervin 2011; 2006; 2005). The data come from self-reflective, in-depth interviews completed by students in classes at two Midwestern United States universities. Some further interviews of relatives, friends and other contacts were conducted. (In all cases, data are used only from informants for whom permission was obtained.) The particular examples used here have been selected because they exemplify specific themes. The modes of data collection and nature of the interviews are typical of the several thousand cases we have collected focusing on lay-person encounters with works of art, ranging from popular culture to so-called 'elite' culture. This large sample, when analysed demographically, closely mirrors the profile of the Midwestern population in terms of ethnicity, education and socio-economic class.

Central to our data collection is the use of Dervin's Sense-Making Methodology (SMM) both as interviewing approach and as meta-theoretic guide for research design and analysis. SMM has now had forty years of development and is widely cited in audience studies of all kinds, including users of information systems, audiences of all forms of media, citizen understandings of public policy and patients interacting with health-care systems, among others (Dervin & Foreman-Wernet 2003).

Where SMM most visibly impacts research is in implementation of how it informs interviewing practice. The approach is informed by a host of philosophically oriented scientists and humanists (Dervin 2003) and owes a particular debt to the work of Richard F. Carter (2003).

The Sense-Making Methodology starts with central assumptions about the nature of humans, knowing, experience and sense-making. Humans, SMM assumes, are mandated by the human condition to move through a time-space ('reality') that is at least in part chaotic (constantly changing, incomplete), surrounded by multiple interpretations of that reality that are themselves at least in part chaotic (constantly changing, incomplete and in contention). SMM assumes that humans are always mandated to 'make sense' – that is, take the next step cognitively, emotionally, physically, spiritually – in the absence of complete instruction. Sometimes this step is robotic or habitual, sometimes is seen by the actor as constrained by external forces; sometimes inventive, sometimes coherent and articulated; sometimes not. SMM further assumes that informants are able to articulate at least in part their moves and stops, successes and failures and link these to both internal and external changing conditions.

The Sense-Making Methodology also assumes that everyday exchanges between humans (experts to lay; lay to lay) are bounded by communicative hegemonies. What we mostly get from usual exchanges is pictures of stereotypic and habitual behaviour but not the narratives, hopes and dreams, challenges and struggles that make up the core of human experiencing and are so central to human appreciations of art. Our data have consistently shown yawning gaps between, for example, the assumptions of arts institutions and the experiences (often profound) of everyday persons. This same expert-lay gap has been exhibited in every field to which SMM has been applied.

The SMM interview is philosophically designed to systematically break through this veil of hegemonies. While a variety of different approaches to the SMM interview bracket time-space in different ways, all are designed to elicit deep self-reflections from informants that have not yet been articulated, but show how each person's experience is both centred and de-centred; sometimes changing and sometimes with a stable centre.

The SMM interview always uses the same core series of queries relating to each informant's encounter. The SMM core questions are:

1. What conclusions, thoughts, insights did you come to?
2. What confusions, questions did you experience?
3. What emotions, feelings did you have?
4. How did this relate to your past experience?
5. Did this help?
6. Did it hinder?
7. Did it relate to your sense of self in any way?
8. Did it relate to how you see power or constraining structures as operating in your life, community, family, society?

Depending on the interviewing approach, this set of core SMM questions is applied repetitively to differing aspects of the informant's sense-makings as these change in movements through time-space. In this way, informants are encouraged and facilitated in sharing deeper and deeper self-reflections.

General findings

Analysis of data collected over the past dozen years of our *Sense-Making the Arts* project has produced a number of themes of patterned response to individual encounters with the arts. While we have looked at audience experiences across the cultural spectrum (Foreman-Wernet & Dervin 2011; 2006; 2005), we limit our discussion here to the performing arts. We note that the beneficial outcomes of arts experiences that have been identified by our informants are also precisely the ones that are discussed in the aesthetics literature and are well understood by lovers of the arts. Not all outcomes are beneficial, however; our informants also identified arts experiences that had negative or mixed outcomes. We discuss these themes and provide illustrative quotes from our research below.

Truth/Beauty

The arts are often understood by our lay informants to convey beauty and a valid way of knowing; something that is particularly special or true and characterized by perfection or purity. At times this truth or beauty has been so intense that it resulted in what might be described as a spiritual experience when informants said they were able to connect to something greater than themselves, the phenomenon that in aesthetics is often called the sublime, or transcendence:

> My emotions were running on high. I was in awe of how the performers' voices and motions just flowed with the music of the orchestra. I lived it. I could not grasp how so many things could be pulled together to make something so beautiful.
>
> (Female, early twenties, *Phantom of the Opera*)

> I felt a total thrill. The music and the dancing were so incredibly beautiful that I just got lost in them; it was very peaceful, too … It seemed to be the epitome of beauty and grace, the images and the sound combined to produce a magical feeling.
>
> (Female, early twenties, *Sleeping Beauty*)

Captivation

Our informants have told us repeatedly that arts experiences have the ability to captivate them, to cause them to become 'lost' in the moment or to be so enthralled that they lose track of time and place:

> In this case, the music that was played caught my attention in such a way that I got this tunnel vision and I noticed nothing else besides the sounds. Nothing has ever caught my attention that quickly before.
>
> (Male, early twenties, orchestral concert)

> The whole experience was something I will never forget … The music was so powerful and true that you could feel it inside. At the close of the final scene, tears were rolling down my face. I found myself with my mouth hanging wide open in amazement. The musical had me so engrossed that my surroundings were invisible.
>
> (Female, mid-twenties, *Phantom of the Opera*)

Self-expression

Our informants have also shared how the arts have facilitated their capacities for self-expression:

> This event awakened my inner soul that was once so in tune with dancing, and brought out many emotions. I think dance is such a beautiful expression of art ... I used to take many dance classes while I was growing up. Even now, it feels so good to dance. I feel absolutely alive! ... It makes me want to get back into dancing.
>
> (Female, early twenties, Alvin Ailey)

> It kind of reminded me of when I used to be in a band when I was younger and played the flute ... I think that by playing an instrument you have some power because you are able to express things through music and bring out ideas and emotions in others.
>
> (Female, early twenties, orchestral concert)

Self-awareness

Experiences with the arts also led our informants to opportunities to develop greater awareness and understanding of themselves:

> I worry constantly and get worked up about things that I shouldn't, so watching and hearing this music made me think of a lot of things that I need to change ... [I realized how] important it is to learn new things and not be afraid to take chances in life. Life is too short to acquire your habits to things you are comfortable with.
>
> (Female, early twenties, *Carmina Burana*)

> I think it made me really think about how I felt about what was going on in my life, which respectively helped me figure out what I wanted to stay the same and what I wanted to change.
>
> (Female, early twenties, Alvin Ailey)

Cognitive/Intellectual growth

Our informants also told us that arts experiences helped them think more fully about the world around them, and to develop new skills and knowledge:

> Since it was only music, I had to use my imagination more to figure out what was going on throughout the songs they played ... I was able to put my imagination to use and make

up a story that went with the music. I also felt absorbed in the music because it was all I had to tell me what was going on.

(Female, early twenties, orchestral concert)

The whole play is about a power struggle between two people, and it made me think about my friends and how we all act toward each other … Helped me realize that people don't want to be around someone that acts so mean. I now think more about my actions.

(Female, early twenties, *Wicked*)

Community/Connection

Arts and cultural activities also provided opportunities for social bonding in a variety of ways. Our informants made frequent references to their attendance at arts events with family members, for example, and at times they articulated connections they felt with their cultural heritages or broader communities:

I think that I gained a better understanding of classical music as I do each time I go to one of my mothers' performances … I also think it helped me because I don't often feel too connected to my mother. I'm extremely close with my father and I think my mother feels isolated sometimes. This gave me a chance to really focus on her and the amazing qualities that she has and why I'm proud to be her daughter.

(Female, early twenties, Monteverdi's *Vespers*)

This play brought about a lot of changes in me and made me have a different outlook on life. It made me want to form a closer bond with my community by making contributions to those less fortunate than myself … Seeing this made me want to do more research on my heritage and do more to try to bring about unity among African American people … It made me want to become active in my community.

(Female, early twenties, *The Life of Frederick Douglas*)

Well-being

Our informants often commented that their experiences with the arts made them happy and resulted in an overall sense of well-being, of pleasure and relaxation:

I was happy when I watched this, knowing many people who were beginning to graduate from college. I could relate to the sentiments it was describing, and it was so funny I couldn't help but be happy while watching it.

(Female, early twenties, *Avenue Q*)

After hearing the music, I felt as calm as I used to feel when I took yoga … I couldn't help but think of why it took an assignment such as this to make me sit down and take some time to myself to actually relax and not worry about anything else that is going on around me.

(Female, early twenties, *Carmina Burana*)

Social judgment

Our informants also explained how engagements with the arts and culture have often led them to draw comparisons between themselves and others – or to confront comparisons, such as stereotypes, drawn by others:

I was able to look at the men on stage and, for the first time, internalize the idea that other boys and men had been feeding me: that men who dance and dress in tights and puffy shirts are sissies.

(Male, early twenties, *The Nutcracker*)

I felt out of place and ignorant. All of my previous experiences with this type of performance shaped what I thought this ballet was supposed to be like and when I saw that it wasn't, I felt very out of place. I couldn't seem to wrap my head around the purpose of the ballet. I didn't understand the overall meaning behind it.

(Female, early twenties, ballet performance)

Case study

In order to provide greater insight into how non-expert audience members of the performing arts actually make sense of their experiences within the context of their lives, we offer a brief case study example.

This case study presents a look at informants' responses to a single event; an online performance of Beethoven's Piano Concerto #5. We purposefully chose a performance that was 'accessible' both in the musical sense and was also offered in a familiar medium that students could watch at their own convenience in places of their choice. We believe this accessibility allowed our informants, whose lives are permeated by popular culture, to engage more reflectively with the experience of classical music. While this small study involved only ten student informants, their self-interviews were especially deep and some clear patterns emerged.

Overwhelmingly our informants had positive responses to the experience, speaking in terms of emotional well-being and how they were drawn into the experience:

I am really impressed with how upbeat and inspiring this music is. I have feelings of joy. It makes me want to invent stuff or fly or something.

(Male, mid-twenties)

I was engulfed in the performance and amazed by the pianist ... I felt really involved in the performance and almost in a trance watching the pianist play the piano with such force and enthusiasm during some parts and with a calm and delicate manner during other parts of the performance. Because of these differences throughout it I also felt excited and enthusiastic at times and calm and relaxed at other times.

(Female, early twenties)

A number of informants also discussed the experience in terms of its beauty:

It helped remind me of the beauty of classical music and showed me just what humans are capable of.

(Male, mid-twenties)

I thought it was beautiful, and very grand and epic. I'm impressed that people can perform (and conduct) like that; it takes so much dedication and talent. People devote their lives to music, but clearly it matters, because this piece, for example, is still being played after all this time ... Why exactly does music have such a power over us? As much as science tries – it can identify as many brain receptors lighting up as it pleases – it can never completely explain the way music and stories and art moves us.

(Female, early twenties)

A major theme in this case study was that our informants expressed surprise that they liked this experience, wondered why they had not listened to classical music before (or why they got away from listening to it) and lamented that mainstream culture and the social judgment of peer pressure discouraged them from doing so. What is more, because of this positive experience, many articulated their desire to seek out more classical music to listen to in the future:

Wow, I have never given much respect or thought to this classical music genre, but this was actually very delightful music ... Why haven't I been introduced to this music before? ... I have often been told that classical music is boring or not 'great' music. I'm disappointed that I let other people's point of view distort my taste in music ... This music definitely changed my opinion on the genre, not to mention I will be listening to this stuff more than I have.

(Female, early twenties)

I felt attached to the performance more and more as it went on. The way the music was played had me hooked and, like a book, I just couldn't put it down, or in this case stop listening. I was excited to hear what was next because the performance is so dynamic ... I'm excited and anxious to explore the classical genre after viewing this cultural product.

(Male, early twenties)

In addition to insights into the social pressure of their peers, the impact of social judgments was also evident in some informants' comments regarding the perceived elitist nature of classical music:

> I believe only the elite really enjoy this type of music … Why do I not like the elite? Was it because I'm from a middle class family? Is it because I work at a country club and get to see first hand how crumby some of the elite can be?
>
> (Male, mid-twenties)

> The piece was being played in what looked like an expensive place and probably only the wealthy went to it. I grew up in a middle class home and we did not really have the taste to go see something like this. I feel like people who go to these have money.
>
> (Male, early twenties)

Our informants also grounded this experience in their understandings of themselves and their aspirations:

> I will now open up my palate for more music to enter my life … I'm excited for the opportunity to learn more about myself … [I]t not only changed my view on this genre of music but also how I felt about a lot of things I had negative views about.
>
> (Female, early twenties)

> It related to how I enjoy classical music and how I see myself as somewhat refined and able to enjoy something like this. I didn't think of it in an arrogant or condescending way, rather just that most of my friends don't enjoy this music.
>
> (Male, mid-twenties)

Our informants in some interviews also talked about the positive impacts of the experience in terms of cognitive or intellectual growth, sometimes couched in the idea of being 'well rounded':

> It showed me that it doesn't necessarily take a trained ear to appreciate classical music, but such rich sounds can be enjoyed by most anyone who takes the time to listen and appreciate.
>
> (Female, early twenties)

> It helped in a sense I'm expanding my musical knowledge … I enjoy music so it was nice to listen to a different type. I say I like to try new things and I did … [I felt] happiness. I love music. What other music is out there that I'm missing out on?
>
> (Male, mid-twenties)

In a few cases, our informants framed their experiences by talking about their connections with family members and significant others:

> I don't know that much about classical music, though I have heard some of it growing up. My parents have a really varied taste in music; when I think of my dad I think of both Led Zeppelin and Bach pipe organ pieces shaking the speakers in our living room.
> (Female, early twenties)

> It reminded me of being little and listening to this music with my grandma who first introduced me to it and took me back to the feelings I had as a little girl spending time with her.
> (Female, early twenties)

Finally, many of our informants commented on the performance itself, saying they were impressed with the talent, skill and dedication of the musicians. A few also asked questions or made comments specific to this performance:

> Why did Beethoven originally write this? And when did it start to become popular to pair lyrics with music? ... I looked it up, 1811 ... I went and looked up the answer so it helped me gain knowledge ... I didn't think I could like music made in the 1800s, but I was wrong ... I'm someone who likes to know the answers, so I had to go and Wikipedia Beethoven's 5th piano concerto ... I wonder if going to a concert in 1811 was anything like going to a concert now?
> (Male, mid-twenties)

> Is there a meaning behind Beethoven's 5th piano concerto? How difficult is it to learn such an elaborate piece of work? Because I'm not too familiar with classical music, I wasn't sure if all pieces of music like this one are separated into parts or if it is unique ...
> (Male, early twenties)

In summary, our interviews revealed that informants experienced both positive and negative aspects of this performance. They talked about the hindrances of social judgment in terms of peer pressure and elitism. But they were also able to tap into what the literature has traditionally advanced as the positive impacts of the arts. They experienced beauty, captivation, well-being, self-awareness and cognitive growth. Indeed, the experience was so positive that many said they were motivated to seek out more classical music experiences.

Conclusion

This chapter has offered a contribution to the expanding body of qualitative research that seeks to better understand how audience members actually experience arts performances. Our approach was based on Dervin's Sense-Making Methodology (SMM), which allowed us – and our informants – to delve more deeply into the interpretive process. SMM interviews provided our informants a means to engage in more reflective thinking about their experiences and allowed them to break through surface-level responses to articulate aspects of their experiences that were both helpful and hindering, that connected to their understandings of themselves and the worlds around them, and that were anchored in their everyday lives.

In keeping with the positive impacts of the performing arts that have been identified in the literature and by patrons of the arts, our informants have been able to tap into aesthetic truth and beauty; have been captivated by performances; have gained self-awareness; have been facilitated in self-expression; have grown cognitively or intellectually; have connected with friends, family and community; and have reported feelings of happiness and well-being.

Our informants have also identified negative impacts related to their performing arts experiences, which to large degree – since our informants' lives are enmeshed in popular culture – we would cast as barriers to engaging with the performing arts. For many of them, engaging with the performing arts was an option that never even crossed their minds. In the popular culture world – and thus in the everyday worlds of our informants – the classical performing arts are rarely mentioned, and if so they are routinely cast with negative associations such as 'not cool' or 'elitist'. As illustrated in our case study, however, when they were encouraged to watch a performing arts event, many of our informants were pleasantly surprised by how much they enjoyed the experience. They were disappointed that because of a lack of awareness or peer pressure they had not engaged in similar experiences before. Many of them vowed to seek out more of Beethoven's music or more classical music in general.

Some of our informants, both in our ongoing research project and also in the case study presented here, also shared their perceptions of the performing arts as elitist, as not intended for less wealthy or less educated people. At times, as noted above, this perception was refuted in our informants' interviews, but it nonetheless is understood by many as a valid issue. We would argue the problem of elitism is an ongoing barrier to traditional arts participation (Foreman-Wernet 2010).

Our findings of impacts – both positive and negative – on audiences from their encounters with the performing arts suggest three important action implications. First, performing arts institutions need to continue to find creative ways to break through the clutter of popular culture so that the performing arts can enter the consciousness of potential audiences. Second, performing arts institutions need to address the issue of accessibility – psychological (presented in a non-threatening way), physical (at convenient times and locations) and aesthetic (at least somewhat familiar, but not 'dumbed down' as illustrated by the Beethoven example). Third, performing arts institutions need to help audience members, especially those new to the performing arts, to make sense of their arts experiences and to assist them in connecting these with their everyday lives in meaningful ways so that they can plumb the rich and rewarding impacts of the performing arts that so many lovers of the arts advocate.

Our research findings across studies have convinced us that even novice audience members are ready and able to travel this journey. The next step in our long-term research project is to design and test procedures that will allow these implementations.

References

Balfe, J. H. (2003), 'Public Participation in the Arts and Culture', in V. B. Morris & D. B. Pankratz (eds), *The Arts in a New Millennium: Research and the Arts Sector* Westport, CN: Praeger, pp. 51–63.

Balfe, J. H., & Peters, M. (2000), 'Public Involvement in the Arts', in J. M. Cherbo & M. J. Wyszomirski (eds), *The Public Life of the Arts in America*, New Brunswick, NJ: Rutgers University Press, pp. 81–98.

Belfiore, E. & Bennett, O. (2007), 'Determinants of Impact: Towards a Better Understanding of Encounters with the Arts', *Cultural Trends,* 16: 3, pp. 225–275.

Bradford, G., Gary, M. and Wallach, G. (eds) (2000), *The Politics of Culture: Policy Perspectives for Individuals, Institutions, and Communities.* New York: New Press.

Brown, A. S. (2004), *The Values Study: Rediscovering the Meaning and Value of Arts Participation,* Connecticut: Commission on Culture and Tourism, Arts Division.

Brown, A. S. & Novak, J. L. (2007), *Assessing the Intrinsic Impacts of a Live Performance,* WolfBrown, http://www.wolfbrown.com/mups_downloads/Impact_Study_Final_Version_full.pdf. (accessed 10 March 2011).

Carter, R. F. (2003), 'Communication, a Harder Science', in B. Dervin & S. Chaffee with L. Foreman-Wernet (eds), *Communication, A Different Kind of Horse Race: Essays Honoring Richard F. Carter,* Cresskill, NJ: Hampton Press, pp. 369–376.

Chartrand, H.H. (1998), 'Art and the Public Purpose: The Economics of it All', *Journal of Arts Management, Law and Society,* 28: 2, pp. 109–113.

Cheney, T. (2010), 'Art and Me: The Personal Presence of Art, its Significance to a Society, and its Relevance to Government Culture Policies', in L. Foreman-Wernet & B. Dervin (eds), *Audiences and the Arts: Communication Perspectives,* Cresskill, NJ: Hampton, pp. 61–74.

Cherbo, J. M. (1998), 'The Arts Sector: Introduction', *Journal of Arts Management, Law and Society,* 28: 2, pp. 99–101.

DeNora, T. (2000), *Music in Everyday Life,* Cambridge, UK: Cambridge University Press.

Dervin, B. (2003), 'Sense-Making's Journey from Metatheory to Methodology to Method', in B. Dervin & L. Foreman-Wernet, *Sense-Making Methodology Reader: Selected Writings of Brenda Dervin,* Cresskill, NJ: Hampton Press, pp. 133–264.

———— (2008), 'Interviewing as Dialectical Practice: Sense-Making Methodology as Exemplar', paper delivered at *International Association of Media and Communication Research, Stockholm, Sweden,* July 20–25, 2008, available from: dervin.1@osu.edu.

Dervin, B. & Foreman-Wernet, L., *Sense-Making Methodology Reader: Selected Writings of Brenda Dervin,* Cresskill, NJ: Hampton Press, 2003.

Florida, R. (2002), *The Rise of the Creative Class and How It's Transforming Work, Leisure, Community and Everyday Life*. New York: Basic Books.

Foreman-Wernet, L. (2010), 'Targeting the Arts Audience: Questioning Our Aim(s)', in L. Foreman-Wernet & B. Dervin (eds), *Audiences and the Arts: Communication Perspectives*, Cresskill, NJ: Hampton Press, pp. 21–41.

Foreman-Wernet, L. & Dervin, B. (2005), 'Comparing Arts and Popular Culture Experiences: Applying a Common Methodological Framework', *Journal of Arts Management, Law, and Society*, 35: 3, pp. 169–187.

—— (2006), 'Listening to Learn: "Inactive" Publics of the Arts as Exemplar', *Public Relations Review*, 32: 3, pp. 287–294.

—— (eds) (2010), *Audiences and the Arts: Communication Perspectives*, Cresskill, NJ, Hampton Press.

—— (2011), 'Cultural Experience in Context: Sense-Making the Arts', *Journal of Arts Management, Law, and Society*, 41: 1, pp. 1–37.

Hunter, J. D. (1991), *Culture Wars: The Struggle to Define America*, New York: Basic Books.

Ivey, B. (2008), *Arts, Inc.: How Greed and Neglect Have Destroyed Our Cultural Rights*, Berkeley: University of California Press.

Jackson, M.-R. J. & Herranz, J. J. (2002), *Culture Counts in Communities: A Framework for Measurement*, Washington, DC: Urban Institute.

McCarthy, K., Ondaatje, E., Zakaras, L. & Brooks, A. (2004), *Gifts of the Muse: Reframing the Debate about the Benefits of the Arts*, Santa Monica, CA: Rand.

Mulcahy, K. V. (2006), 'Cultural Policy: Definitions and Theoretical Approaches', *Journal of Arts Management, Law, and Society*, 35: 4, pp. 319–330.

Pitts, S. & Spencer, C. P. (2008), 'Loyalty and Longevity in Audience Listening: Investigating Experiences of Attendance at a Chamber Music Festival', *Music & Letters*, 89: 2, pp. 227–238.

Postman, N. *Amusing Ourselves to Death: Public Discourse in the Age of Show Business*, New York: Viking Press, 1986.

Radbourne, J., Glow, H. & Johanson, K. (2010), 'Measuring the Intrinsic Benefits of Arts Attendance', *Cultural Trends*, 19: 4, pp. 307–324.

Radbourne, J., Johanson, K., Glow, H., & White, T. (2009), 'The Audience Experience: Measuring Quality in the Performing Arts', *International Journal of Arts Management*, 11: 3, pp. 16–29.

Rumbold, K. (2008), 'The Arts Council England's "Arts Debate"', *Cultural Trends*, 17: 3, pp. 189–195.

Stevenson, D., Rowe, D. & McKay, K. (2010), 'Convergence in British Cultural Policy: The Social, the Cultural, and the Economic', *Journal of Arts Management, Law & Society*, 40: 4, pp. 248–265.

Wali, A., & Ostergaard, J. (2010), 'Toward a More Inclusive Approach to Participation: The Varieties of Art Experiences', in L. Foreman-Wernet & B. Dervin (eds), *Audiences and the Arts: Communication Perspectives*, Cresskill, NJ: Hampton Press, pp. 43–60.

White, T. R. & Hede, A.-M. (2008), 'Using Narrative Inquiry to Explore the Impact of Art on Individuals', *Journal of Arts Management, Law & Society*, 38: 1, pp. 19–36.

Wyszomirski, M. J. (2000), 'Raison d'Etat, Raisons des Arts: Thinking about Public Purposes', in J. M. Cherbo & M. J. Wyszomirski (eds), *The Public Life of the Arts in America*, New Brunswick, NJ: Rutgers University Press, pp. 50–78.

Note

1   Among the factors influencing these shifts have been the dominance of mass media and entertainment culture (see, e.g., Postman 1986) the so-called 'culture wars' (see, e.g., Hunter 1991) and increasing interest in more broadly defined creative activity (see, e.g., Florida 2002). For an overview discussion of issues related to arts and cultural policy in the United States, see Bradford et al. (2000).

Chapter 6

Amateurs as Audiences: Reciprocal Relationships between Playing and Listening to Music

Stephanie E. Pitts

Empirical studies of audience members at classical concerts regularly focus on the attendance habits, musical preferences and socio-economic status of those listeners, but more rarely consider the role of past or current playing of an instrument in shaping concert attendance and engagement. Research on the impact of instrumental learning, likewise, tends to overlook the ways in which acquiring instrumental or vocal skills affects not just future performance activity, but also long-term engagement in music listening. In music education, arts management and performance practice, therefore, the interaction between performing and listening is usually understood as a process of delivery from expert performer to receptive listener, without much acknowledgement of the effects that even minimal prior experience of instrumental playing might have on a listener's perspective.

Among a chamber music audience, a listener with memories of attempting to learn the violin in childhood is likely to hear the virtuosic melodies of a Haydn string quartet differently from one who has never played an instrument; admiring the successful execution of tricky passages but perhaps being more critical of the occasional misplaced intonation. A drummer accustomed to improvising with jazz musicians might observe and appreciate the skill of the jazz group playing background music at a wedding reception – maybe finding it a distraction from the food and conversation also on offer. Anecdotal evidence exists in abundance for the effects – both positive and negative – of performing experience on audience listening, but few studies have examined these effects in detail. This chapter returns to studies of audience experience carried out with jazz and classical listeners in the United Kingdom to uncover insight on the reciprocal relationships between playing and listening to music, aiming to clarify the interesting questions surrounding this topic, and to suggest ways in which they might be more thoroughly investigated.

Performers as listeners

Learning from listening tends to be a peripheral aspect of a musician's training and professional development: Stewart Gordon's (2006) guide to *Mastering the Art of Performance* makes no reference to listening or concert-going, while Gerald Klickstein (2009: 98) gives only a brief mention of the need to 'listen and listen until you break through to the soul of a style', adding that, through recordings and live performances, a player can learn to recognize 'the gestures that composers write and the spin that performers add'. Pianist and musicologist

Peter Hill cautions against listening to recordings too early in the process of learning a new piece of music, suggesting that this 'should be kept to a later stage of study when one is better placed to make an independent critical assessment' (Hill 2002: 143). In each of these instances, performers are urged (sometimes cautiously) to listen for a specific purpose – to understand a composer's style, or a pianist's expressive decisions – in the same way that aspiring writers of fiction are encouraged to 'read closely, word by word, sentence by sentence, pondering each deceptively minor decision the writer [has] made' (Prose 2006: 3). Being a performer, in these examples, implies a particular approach to listening, which might be difficult to suspend in order to listen 'innocently' for pure enjoyment.

Some research has suggested that musicians (and musicologists) listen differently, engaging in 'syntactic' listening whereby the composer's decisions are perceived as the music unfolds: '[Syntactic listening] involves an ability to "go along" with a composer, to engage vicariously in his or her craft – posing a problem, solving it, denying expectations and then fulfilling them, and so on' (Kemp 1996: 129). This approach is encouraged in the teaching of music history and analysis, where 'the discipline of the musical structure has become the norm of both musical academia and (in milder form, perhaps) the concert hall – and the result is a style of listening that has technical focus, specificity, and adherence to the particular work as virtues' (Clarke 2005: 135).

Neuroscience provides some evidence for the distinctiveness of the performer's approach to listening, with recent studies observing differences in brain structure (Gaser & Schlaug 2003) and auditory processing (Seung et al. 2005) between individuals with or without musical training. Lauren Stewart's (2008) review of the literature on musicians' brains reports that listening to music activates neurological pathways associated with performing experience; so singers resting their voices are advised not to listen to music 'in order to avoid straining the voice through automatic subvocalisation', and pianists' brains show a different response when they listen to music that they have played on the piano, as compared with a flute piece for which they do not have a physical muscle memory (Stewart 2008: 306). As Eric Clarke points out, however, attentive listening (of the kind musicians are likely to demonstrate during psychological experiments), stereotyped as 'silent, stationary, uninterrupted, ears glued to the musical structure and eyes closed' (Clarke 2005: 136), is only one approach to hearing music, taking its place among the distractions, social interactions and fluctuating engagement of most concert hall listening.

The effects of musical training on listening are not necessarily positive, sometimes making listeners feel excessively critical and unable to engage emotionally with a concert performance. The pianist Susan Tomes has written of the 'fine line between the state of knowledge which allows you to appreciate something immensely, and the state of expertness which means that you know too much to be able to "suspend disbelief", as they say about theatre' (Tomes 2010: 85). While occasionally Tomes finds her insight on the process of making music to be 'a piece of good fortune which equips me to be the happiest person in the audience', more often her insider knowledge is a source of tension in listening, as she feels 'condemned to see the inner workings, the loose threads, all the bits they forgot to include'. Elizabeth Hellmuth

Margulis has demonstrated that programme notes can cause a similar effect for untrained listeners by making listening more conceptual and less instinctive: in her study, 'short text descriptions, whether dramatic or structural, reduced enjoyment in everyday listeners for 45 [second] excerpts from Beethoven String Quartets', so undermining the assumption of programme note writers that providing listeners with more information will necessarily be an aid to listening (Margulis 2010: 298). As Tomes puts it, understanding music from the inside makes 'listening to other people's performances ... more and more satisfying, until suddenly it isn't' (Tomes 2010: 85).

Mary Dullea, also a concert pianist, reflects similarly on the performer's heightened experience of listening, but finds that a conscious effort 'to prepare, even for a minute, by slowing everything down and just letting myself, my ears and my mind be part of the experience' allows her to 'register these thoughts but not allow them to impede the remainder of the performance' (Personal communication, 2011). This strategy is a familiar one from the control of performance anxiety, whereby performers learn to 'become more closely familiar with parts of their performance that are within their control, and can interrupt or distance themselves from worries that stem from sources beyond their control' (Connolly & Williamon 2004: 233). Dullea's description of working to achieve focus as a listener shows that being in an audience can be effortful as well as enjoyable – a fact that performers might be particularly keen to acknowledge, given the hours of work involved in preparing music for public performance.

For amateurs as well as professionals, being actively involved in making music can reduce the time available for music listening: documenting his learning of the cello as an adult, Wayne Booth (1999: 150) writes of the 'radical sacrifice' of choosing to spend his time playing chamber music at an amateur level rather than listening to professional recordings of the same works. Beyond the satisfaction of playing, he reports that his listening too has been transformed: 'learning to play, or trying to learn to play, is the best step towards deeper listening' (Booth 1999: 151). Similarly, in an investigation of music researchers' engagement in music, Clemens Wöllner and colleagues (2011: 371) found that respondents valued 'active listening' highly, but the majority (72%) engaged in this activity for under four hours a week, with one respondent declaring a deliberate decision to undertake a musical 'diet' and 'choose stillness instead'. The researchers describe as 'inevitable' the response that for a musically trained listener, background listening is impossible since 'it immediately becomes an active listening process' (Wöllner et al. 2011: 371). This means that the engagement with music in daily life widely reported in other studies (e.g., DeNora 2000; Sloboda et al. 2001) is experienced differently by trained musicians – a topic worth further investigation for the insight it would provide on the relationships between musical materials, listeners' perspectives and the emotional functions of music (cf. Clarke 2005).

Finally in this review of literature, the distinctiveness of the amateur musician's perspective on listening is further demonstrated by accounts of musical participation, in which listening is shown to be a source of inspiration, motivation and occasional rivalry for performers (Pitts 2005a). Liz Garnett (2005) and Robert Stebbins (1996) have both explored the world of barbershop singing, in which competitive festivals regularly provide the opportunity for singers to compare their own performances with those of other groups. Under these conditions, with at least half the audience consisting of groups waiting for or returning from their own competition performance, listening becomes 'a vicarious reliving of the performance experience' (Garnett 2005: 62), inviting an empathy with the performers alongside a critique of their performance. For performers of Gilbert and Sullivan operettas, similarly, comparisons with other amateur groups provide a sense of solidarity and community, but in this genre, unlike barbershopping, there is also a professional world to provide a point of inspiration and connection for performer-listeners (Pitts 2009).

In all these instances, it seems that experiential knowledge of performance heightens a listener's awareness of the process of performing, in ways that are sometimes inspiring, sometimes distracting, but always difficult to ignore. Musicians, this published evidence suggests, do listen differently – from different perspectives, and for different reasons – but not necessarily with greater enjoyment than those whose experience of music is mainly acquired through listening. The next section of this chapter examines empirical evidence from audiences at a chamber music festival, in a jazz club and at orchestral concerts, to see how prominent these performer-listeners are in a typical audience, and how much their experience of performing affects their engagement as listeners.

Perspectives from the audience

The audience perspectives provided in this section have been gathered over a range of empirical studies with chamber music listeners (Pitts 2005b; Pitts & Spencer 2008), at a jazz festival (Burland & Pitts 2010) and in a jazz club (ongoing research with Karen Burland), and with the audience for an orchestral concert series (ongoing research with Melissa Dobson and Kate Gee). In each case, a combination of qualitative methods including questionnaires, interviews and diaries was used to explore audience attitudes and loyalty to specific events, performers and genres, with the aim of understanding the appeal and experience of live music for a range of listeners.

In the questionnaire surveys that began each of these projects, respondents were asked about their own level of performing activity: whether they had previously learnt an instrument, whether they still played, alone or with others and, in some of the studies, whether they would describe themselves as a musician. In the first of these studies, carried out at the Music in the Round chamber music festival in Sheffield, in May 2003 (Pitts 2005b), 63 per cent of the 347 respondents reported past or current involvement in playing music – a strikingly high figure that suggests that chamber music attracts an audience with some insider knowledge of the instruments and music being played. However, only 20 per cent of respondents described themselves as musicians, with many others dismissing quite extensive playing activity – including membership of local amateur ensembles – as not being worthy of that title. Typical comments included, 'I'd just about describe myself as a singer but I've never thought as myself as a musician', and '[I'm] musical, rather than a musician.' Nonetheless, musical engagement was highly valued both for its own sake and for the additional insight it brought to respondents' listening, as in the case of the pianist who reported that 'I like to play the piano to understand how the music works, but can't play it for anyone else to listen with pleasure'.

Further insight came in the interviews with these chamber music listeners, where some of the more active performers reflected on making choices between playing and listening (cf. Booth 1999). Jim (all respondent names are pseudonyms), a folk violinist who occasionally played classical chamber music, felt that in a clash between listening to a concert and playing at a paid gig, 'it'd have to be something pretty special to stop me taking the gig – I think I'd tend to go for playing first', although he named specific works and performers for whom he would make an exception. As other audience members made choices about which concerts to attend, their own playing was influential: Alice mainly sought out solo piano recitals since 'having played a little myself, I suppose it just makes it more interesting', and also enjoyed string quartets, explaining that 'I did play in a string quartet sometimes when I was younger, so […] while they're doing it I suppose I can imagine what it's feeling like and how wonderful it is to play without a conductor, and in a very small intimate group'. Paul, another folk violinist, spoke of how his experience of listening to other members of his own ensemble made him more appreciative of performers' musical interaction as an audience member: '[W]hen you've got professionals on the job, you know, it is absolutely astonishing how they can just switch it on and they sort of shut things out and they're in with each other.' Rather than giving him unrealistic expectations of professional performance standards, Paul felt that his playing insight made him more forgiving of small errors: '[Y]ou don't have illusions about you know, oh magnificent, perfection and all the rest of it, because they're human and actually you know that, but their being human is working bloody well [laughs] and you can admire that too.'

This empathy with the performers extended to speculation about their lifestyle and level of musical satisfaction, with the most advanced performer among the audience interviewees, singer Felicity, feeling herself to be more fortunate as a busy semi-professional: 'I know a lot of professional musicians who are very dissatisfied and very bored, and you know, for me music will never ever be boring, it's impossible, so I'm very lucky.' Contemplating the imminent retirement of the festival's host string quartet, Emily and Richard drew parallels with their own experience, recalling the disbanding of an amateur choir in which they had sung for over thirty years, and recognizing 'a kind of sadness in one way, but I think also understanding of a very courageous decision'. In each case, these listeners imagined themselves in the performers' position, sometimes noting the distance between their own music-making and that of the professionals, while finding their playing and listening mutually strengthened through their dual perspectives.

While the Music in the Round audience included a high proportion of singers, pianists and string players with experience of chamber music, audience members at an orchestral concert might be less likely to have had the opportunity to play in a large ensemble, resulting in a different relationship between their own music-making and those of the professionals they listened to. In a study with the City of Birmingham Symphony Orchestra (CBSO) carried out with Melissa Dobson and Kate Gee, we used the participation categories from the Arts Council of England's *Taking Part* survey (Oskala & Bunting 2009) to ask audience members if they engaged in music-making by (a) singing to an audience or rehearsing for a performance, (b) playing a musical instrument to an audience or rehearsing for a performance, and/or (c) playing an instrument or singing for their own pleasure. Singing was described as 'very important' or 'fairly important' by 23 per cent of the 155 CBSO respondents who answered this question, as compared with the national baseline figure of around 4 per cent (Oskala & Bunting 2009: 11). Playing or rehearsing for performance was important to 19 per cent of the CBSO respondents, again much higher than the 3.4 per cent English average. The greatest engagement with music-making, however, both nationally at 11 per cent and for the CBSO respondents at 47 per cent, was playing or singing for their own pleasure – an activity encompassing both playing alone and informal music-making with friends, as was the case for the Music in the Round audience. Being an active performer is perhaps less important therefore than being a *player* of music – someone who engages with making sound and understands the challenges and pleasures of doing so.

For some of the CBSO interviewees, an interest in classical music had been sparked in adolescence by the dual influences of hearing a symphony orchestra live and beginning instrumental lessons – a venture that even when short-lived had given them some insight on the processes of making music. Jenny recalls how she 'went a lot [to CBSO concerts] when I was a teenager because I did music at school, and learnt the clarinet and the piano', suggesting that playing an instrument had heightened her engagement with music, so building foundations for lifelong concert-going. Colin, who had begun his musical life as a trombonist in the local youth orchestra, had also ceased performing in later life, weighing up the balance between playing and listening and finding that he would 'rather go and see music than perform it': as he explains, 'I was never particularly good anyway – so the standard of the orchestras wasn't great, the repertoire was a bit repetitive, you know, you tended to end up doing Brahms symphonies too many times, which I never much enjoyed, and, you know, it took a big lump out of your weekend.' These lapsed musicians were well aware of the gulf between their own playing and that of the professionals they listened to, but like other audience members were convinced of the value of 'catching people when they're young', seeing the educational work of the orchestra as a vital part of sustaining cultural life in their city. Their experiences show the lifelong benefits of even a brief episode of instrumental learning for generating musical insight and engagement, even when active playing is crowded out of adult life by lack of time, progress or inclination.

Another perspective is provided by jazz listeners, for whom an understanding of performer interaction and improvisatory skill is an intrinsic part of attentive listening. Listeners at The Spin jazz club in Oxford (in an ongoing study with Karen Burland) were aware of their contribution to the event, describing in an interview how 'the way that an audience responds can sometimes bring out more from a performer than you might have anticipated happening'.

Both players and non-players in the audience seemed to view their live jazz listening as a learning process, expecting to discover something new about a performer or a well-loved jazz standard with each performance – and for players this knowledge might be applied to their own music-making, at whatever level, in the weeks after the gig. Jazz guitarists, drummers or saxophonists sought out their own instrument when selecting gigs, and enjoyed the experience of sitting 'slack-jawed and drooling' in the presence of a legendary performer. Despite their enjoyment of listening, however, they described gaining 'a certain extra satisfaction from playing', the two activities appearing to stimulate one another in ways that were less common among the classical music listeners, where virtuosity in performers might regrettably be dispiriting rather than motivating to an amateur player.

Conclusions: listeners, players, musicians

The findings in this chapter have emerged almost incidentally from previous studies of audience members' experience, and highlighting the potential for more thorough investigation of this topic. This first exploration has shown how performers – or more accurately, players – among an audience often see themselves as having some additional insight on the musical event, a perspective that might in turn encourage greater attention, or help to direct the focus of listening in ways that enhance the concert experience. Their playing experience shapes their choice of listening, drawing them towards repertoire that they might play themselves – until their playing standards and opportunities reach the point when they would rather be playing the music than listening to it.

Further investigation of the performer/player perspective on listening would need to take a lifespan approach, considering the role of live music listening in inspiring and sustaining musical engagement, from choice of instrument through to lifelong participation. Careful exploration of music student, amateur and professional attitudes to the value of live listening could help shape strategies for incorporating concert attendance at different levels of music education – with a recognition that even accomplished musicians might need support and persuasion to apply their skills as performers to the related but different task of concentrated listening. And while determining what people actually hear from their concert hall seat can be challenging (cf. Thompson 2006), a finer distinction between levels of playing experience in audience studies could shed new light on questions of musical perception and the effects of training, which would inform many branches of music psychology research.

A clearer understanding of the relationship between playing and listening has implications for musical learning, production and consumption at all levels, with the training of performers as attentive listeners having mutual benefits for those who make and hear live music – and the experiences of those player-listeners offering new insight on how to engage audiences of all levels of expertise and experience. These findings have shown that the reciprocal relationships between playing and listening are not entirely uncomplicated: being a performer can enhance listening, but might also reduce motivation or appreciation, exposing the inner workings of musical communication in a way that is (ironically) craved by non-players but sometimes unhelpful once it is acquired. Perhaps the ideal audience members are the satisfied non-performers, who draw on past experience of playing to inform their current engagement in listening, but without a sense of frustration or regret at not being more actively involved. For others, negotiating the balance between playing and listening can cause emotional interference that needs to be addressed at an individual, educational and musical level, if performers are to be enriched by the playing of other musicians and audiences filled with insightful and appreciative listeners.

Acknowledgements

I gratefully acknowledge the contribution of my research assistants and collaborators in the studies referred to in this chapter: Karen Burland, Stephanie Bramley, Melissa Dobson, Kate Gee and Christopher Spencer. Funding has been provided by the British Academy, the University of Sheffield and the University of Leeds. Thanks are due also to the many respondents in the studies who gave generously of their time and opinions to inform our research.

References

Booth, W. (1999), *For the Love of it: Amateuring and its Rivals*, Chicago: University of Chicago Press.

Burland, K. & Pitts, S. E. (2010), 'Understanding Jazz Audiences: Listening and Learning at the Edinburgh Jazz and Blues Festival', *Journal of New Music Research*, 39: 2, pp. 125–134.

Clarke, E. F. (2005), *Ways of Listening: An Ecological Approach to the Perception of Musical Meaning*, Oxford, Oxford University Press.

Connolly, C. & Williamon, A. (2004), 'Mental Skills Training', in A. Williamon (ed.), *Musical Excellence: Strategies and Techniques to Enhance Performance*, Oxford: Oxford University Press, pp. 221–245.

DeNora, T. (2000), *Music in Everyday Life*, Cambridge: Cambridge University Press.

Garnett, L. (2005), *The British Barbershopper: A Study in Socio-Musical Values*, Aldershot: Ashgate.

Gaser, C. & Schlaug, G. (2003), 'Brain Structures Differ between Musicians and Non-musicians', *Journal of Neuroscience*, 23: 27, 9240–9245.

Gordon, S. (2006), *Mastering the Art of Performance: A Primer for Musicians*, New York: Oxford University Press.

Hill, P. (2002), 'From Score to Sound', in J. Rink (ed.), *Musical Performance: A Guide to Understanding*, Cambridge: Cambridge University Press, pp. 129–143.

Kemp, A. E. (1996), *The Musical Temperament: Psychology and Personality of Musicians*, Oxford: Oxford University Press.

Klickstein, G. (2009), *The Musicians' Way: A Guide to Practice, Performance, and Wellness*, New York: Oxford University Press.

Margulis, E. H. (2010), 'When Program Notes Don't Help: Music Descriptions and Enjoyment', *Psychology of Music*, 38: 3, pp. 285–302.

Oskala, A. & Bunting, C. (2009), *Arts Engagement in England from 2005/06 to 2007/08: Findings from the First Three Years of the Taking Part Survey*, London, Arts Council England, http://www.artscouncil.org.uk/media/uploads/Arts_Engagement_England.pdf. (accessed 28 July 2011).

Pitts, S. E. (2005a), *Valuing Musical Participation*, Aldershot: Ashgate.

―――― (2005b), 'What Makes an Audience? Investigating the Roles and Experiences of Listeners at a Chamber Music Festival', *Music and Letters*, 86: 2, pp 257–269.

―――― (2009), 'Champions and Aficionados: Amateur and Listener Experiences of the Savoy Operas in Performance', in D. Eden & M. Saremba (eds), *The Cambridge Companion to Gilbert and Sullivan*, Cambridge: Cambridge University Press, pp. 190–200.

Pitts, S. E. & Spencer, C. P. (2008), 'Loyalty and Longevity in Audience Listening: Investigating Experiences of Attendance at a Chamber Music Festival', *Music and Letters*, 89: 2, pp. 227–238.

Prose, F. (2006), *Reading Like a Writer*, New York: Harper Perennial.

Seung, Y., Kyong, J., Woo, S., Lee, B. & Lee, K. (2005), 'Brain Activation During Music Listening in Individuals with or without Prior Music Training', *Neuroscience Research*, 52: 4, pp. 323–329.

Sloboda, J. A., O'Neill, S. A. & Ivaldi, A. (2001), 'Functions of Music in Everyday Life: An Exploratory Study Using the Experience Sampling Method', *Musicae Scientiae*, 5: 1, pp. 9–32.

Stebbins, R. A. (1996), *The Barbershop Singer: Inside the Social World of a Musical Hobby*, Toronto: University of Toronto Press.

Stewart, L. (2008), 'Do Musicians have Different Brains?' *Clinical Medicine*, 8: 3, pp. 304–308.

Thompson, S. (2006), 'Audience Responses to a Live Orchestral Concert', *Musicae Scientiae*, 10: 2, pp. 215–244.

Tomes, S. (2010), *Out of Silence: A Pianist's Yearbook*, Woodbridge, Boydell & Brewer.

Wöllner, C., Ginsborg, J. & Williamon, A. (2011), 'Music Researchers' Musical Engagement', *Psychology of Music*, 39: 3, pp. 364–382.

Chapter 7

The Longer Experience: Theatre for Young Audiences
and Enhancing Engagement

Matthew Reason

Picture an audience: imagine row upon row of silent, transfixed faces. Each face is gazing in the same direction, sitting in darkness and in silence, expressions lit by the glow coming from stage or cinema screen. Whether we imagine these expressions to be transfixed, rapt and attentive – or, alternatively, empty and unthinking – the predominant Western conceptualization of the audience is of being there to be entertained. At its most stereotypical, this vision of the audience as passive consumers is most associated with television – part of a wider social concern that watching is replacing doing, seeing replacing experiencing. It might be argued, however, that the theatre audience is just as inactive and submissive. It is possible to suggest that the concept of theatre or art for children situates young people as exactly this kind of audience: passive and disempowered; watchers rather than actors; observers rather than participants; spoken to, rather than speaking.

The hope, of course, is that while outwardly passive an audience is in that moment of watching active in multiple processes, pleasures and engagements as they respond to performance: unravelling the layers between illusion and reality; decoding the staging, technique and craft of what they see; engaging empathetically through the imagination and kinesthetically through the body. As Susan Bennett observes, audiences (including young audiences) 'are trained to be passive in their demonstrated behaviour during a theatrical performance, but to be active in their decoding of the sign systems made available' (1997: 206). The transfixed gaze of the audience denotes a physical passivity, but internally the mind and the imagination are very active.

Even if this is the case, however, it is valid to wonder what happens after the performance has ended. The audience empties out of the darkness of the theatre into the busyness of everyday life and all too often, the process of thinking, feeling and responding to the performance ends abruptly. There is nothing inherently wrong with this. If the audience are entertained for the duration of the performance, it is fabulous. This chapter, however, presents the case that perhaps we should ask for this and more: for enjoyment and engagement in the moment of watching and for a rich post-performance afterlife where the experience reverberates in each spectator's engaged and enduring imagination.

In particular, this chapter argues that greater facilitation is needed to ensure that young people's cultural experiences are enhanced and extended rather than being piecemeal and tokenistic. It argues that young people (with the particular focus on children under eleven) benefit from support to enable them to get the most out of their theatre and other arts encounters. This is not because of an external or educational or instrumental benefit that such support might deliver, but instead to extend and enrich the arts encounter itself. Nor is this perspective based upon pessimism about the competencies and capacities that young audiences bring to theatre, but rather optimism about what can happen if they are actively empowered to develop their own sense of criticality. The discussion here overlaps with the material presented in greater depth in my book, *The Young Audience: Exploring and Enhancing Children's Experience of Theatre* (2010). However, the specific example I present here utilizes material not included in that publication, exploring responses gathered from children who had seen a production of *Echoa*, by French-based Compagnie Arcosm. This chapter will explore contrasting responses to this particular performance before discussing how the insights from my research into young audiences have informed the development of resources intended to enable children and young people to become more critical, active and empowered theatre spectators.

Echoa

My research into young audiences began with a project titled 'Drawing the Theatrical Experience', which sought to gather richly detailed accounts of children's experiences of watching theatre. The openness of this enquiry led me to adopt an open and playful methodology, which was focused around visual arts workshops in which children were asked to respond through drawing and painting to a performance they had just witnessed. During the workshops, myself and the other workshop facilitators would move around the room talking to individual children as they drew, or as they finished a particular picture, asking them to tell us about their drawings and through those drawings of their experiences of the theatre production. Our conversations with the children were again deliberately open, often beginning with a question along the lines of 'Tell me about your drawing.' This was followed by questions or conversation as led by the child, the drawing or the performance being discussed.

From the mass of material that this approach developed I was then able to trace and analyse particular threads describing the nature of the young audience's theatrical experiences. These included a description of how young audiences possess a strong and self-aware (if sometimes latent) theatrical competence; of how while often lacking the vocabulary through which to easily articulate their knowledge, young audiences are able not only to decode stage performances but also to analyse and reflect on their decoding (i.e., to a degree, say *how* they know what they know); finally, young audiences engage with both the illusion and material reality of a performance, interested in both imaginatively completing a story or illusion and in recognizing and appreciating the skill and technique involved in creating that illusion. The initial cycle of workshops for this research took place in 2006 and has been explored in detail elsewhere (Reason 2008; 2010). I later conducted some further research workshops with children following a performance of *Echoa* (Figure 7.1), presented at the 2009 Imaginate Festival in Edinburgh.

Figure 7.1: *Echoa*, by Compagnie Arcosm. (Photo: Paul Delgado).

Created by dancer and choreographer Thomas Guerry and percussionist and composer Camille Rocailleux, *Echoa* was first performed in 2001. Featuring two dancers and two musicians it has since been performed more than 500 times in France and internationally, including touring to the United Kingdom, the United States, Poland, South Korea, Brazil and Japan (for information about Compagnie Arcosm, visit www.mitiki.com). Blurring the boundaries between dance, physical theatre and music, and frequently labelled in press material as 'A *Stomp* for young people', *Echoa* has been hugely successful and gathered extremely positive press reviews from around the world. Kelly Apter in *The Scotsman*, for example, gave the production five stars and wrote:

It's hard to conceive of anyone – of any age – not loving ECHOA. [...] Rarely is contemporary dance so instantly accessible and fun, eliciting peels of giggling laughter from young mouths alongside adult guffaws. Best of all, we're all laughing at the same joke, on the same level. Without saying a single word, the performers draw us into their world and unite us as an audience.

(Apter 2009)

Echoa has been an international hit and is a sophisticated and engaging piece of theatre that, speaking personally, I also hugely enjoyed. However, Apter's first sentence, 'It's hard to conceive of anyone – of any age – not loving ECHOA', is a hostage to fortune, and in the research workshops I carried out after *Echoa* in one Scottish school (with children aged seven to eight years), I came across many children who really did not like the performance at all. In one post-show workshop, for example, Dale commented, 'It was cruel to make us watch it', while Rebecca asserted that the best thing about it was 'when it was over' because then she 'didn't have to watch it anymore'.

While it is difficult to isolate a single common reason why Dale and Rebecca and some of the other participants resisted *Echoa* so strongly, declaring it boring and entirely uninteresting, it is possible to identify several factors at play. For adults one of the memorable and impressive aspects of the production was its virtuosity, the bringing together of movement and music in a manner that invited our appreciation of the craft and precision involved. In her review for Londondance.com, for example, Katie Eynon praised the 'complete synchronicity' of the dancers and the 'flawless rhythm' of the percussion (2010). This admiration for virtuosity in performance from adult reviewers mirrors findings in other research I have conducted with adult audiences, particularly to dance, where spectators appreciate the skill and craft of a performance (Reason and Reynolds 2010: 58–60). On this occasion, however, what was striking was that while a strong admiration for virtuosity occurred in reviews and in my informal post-show conversations with adults who had seen *Echoa*, it was entirely absent from the research conducted with children. There were passing remarks from some children that they would like to drum like the performers, but just as frequent were criticisms about the perceived lack of skill involved:

Researcher: What other words would you use to describe the dancing?
John: Spooky bad dancing, look it's rubbish weird crap bad and un-rehearsed.
Researcher: Un-rehearsed?
John: Cause he hit his head on the table.

In part what is going on here is to do with the particular style of dance in *Echoa*, which was vernacular rather than balletic, which employed elements of the slapstick, but which was nonetheless extremely sophisticated and timed to the second. It appears, however, that for a young audience, a lack of knowledge about how difficult the performance was can make this evidence of skill and craft invisible. As another girl remarked about the dancing, 'Anybody could do it.'

Another challenge for the young audience was the absence of spoken dialogue in *Echoa* along with a lack of clear narrative structure. For children with no significant experience of watching non-narrative forms – aside from television and cinema, most of the children's only previous live theatre experience was of musicals and pantomimes – there was a recurring desire for plot and for dialogue. Asked how he would have improved the production, John, for example, replied, 'They could have put a lot of speaking in.'

These two points, the desire for narrative storyline and a lack of engagement with the craft of the performance, are also noted by Willmar Sauter who discusses how 'younger people are more interested in the fictional story presented on stage, whereas interest in the actors and the staging increases steadily with the age of the spectator' (2003: 118). I have some reservations about the absoluteness of this observation, as previously I have observed young audiences actively engaging in the craft and technique of a performance (particularly of puppets, Reason 2008). However, in this instance and for certain audience members, it was the lack of narrative and over reliance on technique that prompted disinterest and dislike. Of course, the negative and even destructive responses to *Echoa* discussed here were also produced in the context of a range of factors including some far beyond the scope of the theatre experience itself.

For example, it is worth acknowledging that for some of the children the adoption of a position of extreme antipathy in relation to *Echoa* was in part a form of rebellion: against us, the researchers specifically, and adult authority, school and cultural impositions more generally. This then developed into a certain pleasure in the vitriol of condemnation – just as the hatchet-job bad review has a certain macabre pleasure to it – and an escalating form of group cohesion. This is not to say that there was any explicit antagonism between researchers and participants, but rather to observe that just as there is a risk in focus group-based research that participants unconsciously look to say things to please the researcher, so with this particular demographic the reverse can be the case. Does this mean that the children did not necessarily mean what they said? Certainly it is possible that these positions of assertive dislike would not necessarily match their feelings and attitude in the moment of watching *Echoa*, but in the post-event reflective construction of the experience they came to predominate.

Nonetheless, it is worth acknowledging that the responses were at least in part produced because the children simply did not make anything of the performance. In some ways the responses were not simply critical, but rather there was no response at all. No reading was made, no meaning or emotion extracted, because the performance was simply irrelevant to their concerns. Yet, at the same time we also recognize the vibrancy and inventiveness of the performance and that for other young spectators it was a fulfilling experience. The question, therefore, becomes that of supporting all audience members in engaging with new and unfamiliar forms; not to change their opinions necessarily but to enable them to make empowered and active responses of their own.

The post-performance experience

The suggestion that an important element of theatre resides in the audience's response to the production is, of course, relatively familiar within performance studies. As is the suggestion that this is not only a momentary engagement but also an ongoing experience that takes place after, as well as during, the event. Sauter, for example, describes theatre as 'an ongoing communicative process, which cannot simply be reduced to the duration of the performance proper' (2003: 120). This perspective is put more evocatively by Eugenio Barba, who writes that 'the performance is the beginning of a longer experience. It is the scorpion's bite which makes one dance. The dance does not stop when you leave the theatre' (1990: 98).

What is particularly useful about Barba's phrase 'a longer experience' is the durational aspect to audiencing that it introduces. Indeed, once accepted that it lasts longer than the performance, the audience experience of a performance can be considered an ongoing, limitless and plural process. As Martin Barker asks (of film rather than theatre) 'when for all practical purposes does the experience end? Of course, on a certain view the only end-point of any experience is death itself. All experiences continue to resonate in one way or another through the life-time of a person' (2006: 135). Barker qualifies this by admitting that this is evidently not literally the case for all experiences: '[I]t is possible to leave a theatre and almost instantly consign the experience to a bin of completed outings.' However, in contrast to this forlorn image of a completed and discarded experience, it is clearly the ongoing experience that is richer and more rewarding. What is interesting, in other words, is not simply whether young audiences are entertained during a performance, but what they take away from it afterwards. What readings do they make? What emotional responses do they have? What connections do they see? How reflective, considered or impulsive are these responses? While a performance is of fixed duration, the post-performance experience can be limitless.

There is a philosophical and aesthetic debate here about the nature of our experience of art, which suggests that as well as the art work or object – and the audience's immediate engagement with the art work – we also need to recognize a longer and ongoing experience. This includes the multiple connotations and interpretations that take place afterwards in audiences' social and imaginative lives after the initial encounter and that formulate as a spectator reflects upon and considers the experience post-performance.

In his 2008 report to the Department of Culture, Media and Sport in the UK, *Supporting Excellence in the Arts*, Brian McMaster writes that 'the best definition of excellence I have heard is that excellence in culture occurs when an experience affects and changes an individual' (2008: 9). With theatre, therefore, what is important is not just what happens on the stage but also what happens within the minds, imagination and memory of the watching audience. One criteria for judgements of quality in theatre of young audiences, therefore, asserts that the quality resides in the experiential response of the audience and not just in the performance.

The difficulty with the responses to *Echoa* that I have been exploring here is that while the production might very well have been excellent (which I am happy to support from my own personal judgement), the experiences of the young audience members was not always of quality.

This was certainly the case with some, but of course not of all, and having explored some of the extremities of dislike that *Echoa* received it is worth presenting an alternative

Figure 7.2: *Echoa* by Teigan.

response, particularly from one girl named Teigan, whose drawing (Figure 7.2) explored and exhibited her sophisticated engagement with the production.

At first glance this drawing is a relatively detailed and fairly literal depiction of the stage appearance of *Echoa*, depicting the scaffolding-like structure at the rear of the stage and the drum sets stage left and right. The real interest, however, comes when Teigan discussed her picture and explained how she drew the musical notes in different colours to represent the different emotions she had associated with the different sections of the performance. Those in the top right hand corner (a reddish purple in the original) were 'sweet', and associated with a scene where a male and female dancer moved slower together on a high table. The notes in the top left (blue in colour) were the sadness that came across in some melancholic xylophone playing. Those down towards the front (yellow) were happiness provoked by a scene when the performers were playing drums in dancing unison. Teigan then explained that when she was watching each bit she was feeling the same emotions: happiness, sadness, sweetness and so on. In this response, Teigan demonstrates skills in interpreting the different meanings projected by the instruments and movements, an empathetic emotional engagement with the moods conveyed and a sophisticated reflective processing in being able to externalize and communicate the nature of her response. It is the response that we might feel this performance, as praised by Kelly Apter, warranted. More crucially, it is the kind of attuned, reflective and engaged response we would want and wish all children to have: it is an experience of quality.

If we start thinking of quality as a criterion of experience as well as of product then we need to think about what can be done to support and ensure this level of engagement.

Enhancing engagement

While conducting these investigations into children's experiences of theatre I became increasingly interested in the ways in which the workshops were not just useful in terms of the research material they produced but also how they actively intervened into the children's experiences and understanding of the performance. They had always been designed to be fun and engaging for the participants but increasingly I was aware that at times they became valuable experiential moments for the children taking part. Put simply, the visual arts workshops themselves became an enriching and enhancing part of the participants' experience of the performance.

This is a fairly common sense observation: if you spend any time reflecting on something, you begin not only to remember more but also start to synthesize the raw encounter into a more consciously articulated experience. Engaging their memories of a production through conversation and drawing required the children to remember more about what they had seen than if they had been left alone. Inevitably at times, participants responded by declaring that they could not remember anything or with other tactics to avoid engaging in conversation. However, much more often the workshops provided participants with structures (drawing and conversation) through which to develop their memories and with active and interested listeners with whom they could share their experiences and interpretations. This encouraged the children to value their own perspectives and to think about what they had seen, to make connections and begin to formulate opinions.

The observation that the post-performance workshops enhanced and extended the participants' engagement with the performance contains the implicit suggestion that unless children are actively encouraged to remember, and to develop and reflect on their memories, then they simply do not. Unless children are invited or actively encouraged to take their processes of engagement with a performance further, it can exist on a limited and momentary level. Now it would be legitimate to argue that this is fair enough; if the audience enjoyed the performances, why should more be necessary? The answer to this is implicit in the contrast between the responses to *Echoa* discussed earlier and in the potential richness of responses that emerge when children have a quality experience that includes a deeper and extended knowledge and sense of ownership of the performance.

From this set of experiences and observations, I came to the conclusion that young audiences can benefit hugely by being provided with the skills and structures through which to extend their encounter with theatre. We need to consider children's continuing engagement with theatre in terms of deepening their knowledge and understanding of their own experience through reflection, analysis and creative play.

Instrumental or intrinsic viewers

At first glance, the objective of seeking to actively enhance and extend young audiences' engagement with theatre performance might seem to be going against a prominent trend in this area, which has been to move away from instrumental perspectives of theatre for young audience that set out to describe what children might get out of the experience. This is a shift described by Katya Johanson and Hilary Glow as being away from instrumental goals that justify children's theatre in terms of its educational benefits and instead towards a valuation of the intrinsic aesthetic rewards of the experience itself (2011). Shifra Schonmann similarly asserts that theatre for children must stop defining itself as an 'education endeavour' and instead concentrate 'on its artistic form and its own aesthetic merits' (2006: 10). I myself argue that theatre for children must always be considered in terms of its strengths as theatre with 'the primary motivation being the enjoyment and reward of the activity itself' (Reason 2010: 40).

The suggestion of a need to actively work to deepen and extend young audiences' engagement with theatre might appear to go against this perspective. To suggest that children need to be 'trained' to become 'better' audiences also seems to undervalue the skills and competencies in spectatorship that young children already have, and to dismiss their perspectives as invalid. Certainly the focus of the enhanced or extended experience should be the theatrical experience, the intrinsic experience and not some educational service existing elsewhere that is accessed through the experience but resides outside of it. Additionally, the objective is not to improve children's taste or to change their minds about what they should like or dislike, but to provide them with the capacities to think critically and to make clear judgements about their own aesthetic preferences.

The ability to engage in reflective dialogue about our arts experiences (whether as adults or as children) is empowering. It places us in greater command of our own experiences; it places the audience in the position of actively interpreting and actively constructing meaning. This ability of knowledge and criticality to give us power and understanding over our own experiences is vital, especially for children. Moreover, this should be a pleasurable position. As Edmund Burke Feldman writes, the pleasure of understanding is one function of art criticism:

We get pleasure from understanding, from knowing what it is in art that causes our gratification. The trained viewer should also be able to experience more of the satisfactions a work is capable of yielding; criticism enables us to carry on the search systematically. The satisfactions we get from art depend on two things: the quality of the object itself, and our capacity to use our own experience in seeing it. So art criticism increases pleasure while teaching us to focus our knowledge and experience in an aesthetic situation.

(Feldman 1995: 469)

For Feldman, art criticism is talk about art that has a degree of informed structure and should form a legitimate and valuable part of young children's art education.

Maxine Greene makes similar points in *Releasing the Imagination* when she describes how informed engagement with the arts 'cannot happen automatically or "naturally"', but instead requires reflective time and dialogue:

The point is that simply being in the presence of art forms is not sufficient to occasion an aesthetic experience or to change a life. Aesthetic experiences require conscious participation in a work, a going out of energy, an ability to notice what is there to be noticed.

(Greene 1995: 125)

The cultivation of an ability to notice, such as that exhibited by Teigan in her clearly active participation with *Echoa*, is the kind of pleasurable and empowering engagement with the intrinsic experience of theatre that needs to be actively encouraged.

To an extent, of course, none of this is new. Productions targeted at young audiences, particularly through school performances, are invariably accompanied by supporting resources and teachers' packs intended to facilitate or deepen the experience. These packs typically suggest activities designed to facilitate the exploration of the themes and characters presented in the production and frequently construct links with key aspects of children's development and learning. Undoubtedly the quality of some of the work produced through engagement with these packs is high, but the extent to which they are adopted and their real benefits or impacts are unknown. Additionally, some commentators have expressed concerns that the focus on fitting into curricula requirements can damage the excellence of the production and the theatrical experience itself. Lyn Gardner, for example, observes: 'I see too many shows whose driving force is clearly not a passion to make theatre, but a passion to sell a product whose major selling point is the way it ties in with the National Curriculum' (2002: 35). My own perception is that the specificity of some production resource packs and the very way they are tailored to particular productions and designed to bring out particular themes is a limiting factor, as they can make watching resemble a decoding exercise of spotting themes and responding accordingly. Such resources have a tendency to flatten and homogenize the experiences and responses produced (other criticisms include Klein 2005).

Resource packs and other conscious efforts to enhance children's engagement can therefore run the risk of educationalizing the experience. At the same time, I have suggested that quality is related to the ambition for richer and more involved engagement in theatre performances. Between these points it seems reasonable that children's experience of theatre should be facilitated in a manner that invites them to engage with the performance in an active, self-reflective and empowered manner, which thereby extends the imaginative and intellectual afterlife of their experiences.

Rather than the specific, narrowing and sometimes closed nature of production resource packs, it is this kind of active, open and self-reflective engagement that we need to encourage and elicit. Our objective should not be in stimulating factual recall, in testing memory or in any direct content orientated curricula, but instead in developing reflection, play, transformation and knowledge. We need to consider what kinds of afterlife a performance has in a child's memory, consider how this afterlife might be extended and ask questions about how children actively play with their experiences – particularly through drawing and conversation. Our understanding should be driven by awareness that engaging children with theatre involves more than simply sitting them down in front of a production – more than simple exposure to the arts – but also a responsibility to contextualize, enhance and frame the experience.

Imaginate: Evaluating the Performing Arts

Much of this research and reflection was conducted in collaboration with Imaginate, an Edinburgh-based organization with the remit to promote and develop the performing arts for children and young people in Scotland. Starting from the core activity of programming a performing arts festival for young audiences, over several years Imaginate has become increasingly interested in the ways in which this work is received and the role of schools and teachers in framing and shaping the audience experience. For many, this interest is accompanied by the perception that teachers often lack the skills required to support the arts effectively. As Martha Taunton notes in the context of arts education at primary school level:

> In part, this difficulty simply stems from a lack of realisation and faith that young children can and should discuss art in a meaningful way, but, in part, it often results from uncertainty about how to conduct discussions about art with children who are so young.
>
> (Taunton 1983: 40)

To address this deficiency, Imaginate has developed learning partnerships with schools and the delivery of high quality professional development for teachers designed to improve skills and understandings around facilitating engagement with the arts. This activity has included working with a teachers' advisory group and other key contributors (including myself) to develop practical resources for teachers and artists interested in the reception of the work they present for young audiences.

In 2010 Imaginate produced two key resources: a publication, *Evaluating the Performing Arts: a Step by Step Teaching Guide*; and an online equivalent, 'Evaluating the Performing

Arts', an interactive resource accessed via Glow, Scotland's (and the world's first) national schools intranet. A key feature of both these resources is a focus on encouraging children to respond in a reflective and critically empowered manner. They are open resources that can be applied to any production and focus not on extraction of content or curricula-related information from a performance but on engagement with the performance on its own terms. As Alice McGrath, development director at Imaginate, writes in the introduction to the published resource, the aim is

> to facilitate discussion and debate, explore the creative process behind a performance and empower teachers and pupils to express their opinions confidently through a variety of means. Most importantly though we hope that through extending engagement with a performance, teachers' and pupils' imaginations are sparked and they feel open to exploring new possibilities.
>
> (McGrath 2010: 4)

The publication *Evaluating the Performing Arts* presents four lesson plans through which to structure post-performance engagement with theatre. The first, 'Playing it Out', uses play and drama games with suggestions as to how practical activities can produce creative responses to a performance. As the resource notes, play is a natural and age appropriate way that children process experiences through which they can take a kind of ownership of the world and of the images presented to them in a performance. Indeed, after watching a performance, children often imitate and repeat scenes, voices or dialogue and through structuring this creative play they can gain an embodied understanding of the work. The second lesson plan, 'Drawing the Theatrical Experience', utilizes the workshop structure developed in my own work to suggest approaches that use the visual arts to externalize experiences and prompt discussion. The value of drawing as a form of visual thinking is something I have explored in detail elsewhere (Reason 2010: 119–35) and as Eileen Adams writes, drawing

> [c]an be used as a tool of enquiry, comprehension and communication. It enables young people to order and understand their experiences, to shape ideas and to communicate their thinking and feeling to others.
>
> (Adams 2002: 222).

The third, 'Talking Theatre Reviews', presents a structure for critical discussions about theatre. This lesson plan was developed from work I conducted with Imaginate and their teachers' advisory group, and also some research into the potential for using P4C approaches (philosophy for children) in the context of a theatre performance (see Reason 2008; 2010: 137–66). The lesson plans note how 'talking about theatre takes us beyond the surface evaluation allowing us to get to the heart of the experience, understanding not only how we were affected, but why we were affected that way'. The final lesson plan,

'Writing Theatre Reviews', was developed in collaboration with theatre critic Mary Brennan and explores the process of writing about a performance. Across each of these structures, while Imaginate stresses the skills in observation, literacy and creativity that enhanced engagement with theatre fosters, the main focus is upon engagement with the experience of the performance itself, inviting more reflective, engaged and self-aware responses. Feedback on the resource, gathered by Imaginate from teachers, includes comments like, 'It has given me new ideas about how to explore the characters, setting and events from stories as well as how to aid recall about performances through drawing'; that they will now try 'using drawing and drama techniques to get pupils to respond to a piece of theatre, a book or a film instead of always expecting a written report'; and that the tools 'support pupils evaluation of performances but also [help in] developing their abilities in evaluation in general'.

The online resource is in a sense an interactive virtual version of the third lesson plan to engage young audiences in the discussion of a performance. It uses an animated theatre critic called Stevie (Figure 7.3) to guide teachers and pupils through a series of structured steps under the headings 'remembering a performance', 'exploring a performance' and 'evaluating a performance'. As the teacher's overview to the resource states:

> This online lesson is led by an animated theatre critic who will guide you and your class through a step by step process of discussing live theatre performance. It is a learning tool designed to develop pupils' ability to evaluate and appreciate live performance.

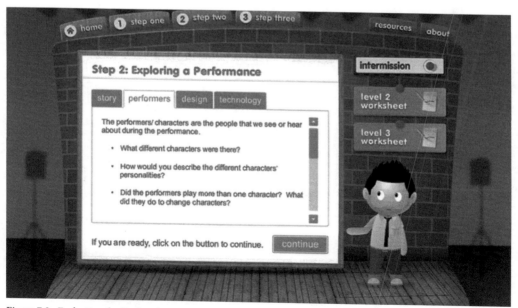

Figure 7.3: Evaluating the Performing Arts Online. Accessed via Glow. (Production: Imaginate).

A cultural co-ordinator working in the Scottish Borders comments that the resource is 'a very accessible and fun way of engaging pupils in the critical evaluation of their theatre experiences. The resource allows teachers and pupils to share/challenge their thoughts and opinions on the performances with other pupils in their class and the wider Glow network.'

Concluding remarks

Helping young audiences to become more active, reflective, critically self-aware and articulate audiences clearly has many instrumental benefits and educational returns. It connects to developing children's capacities in observation, their ability to reason and discuss and externalize ideas.

However, while recognizing that this occurs, the ambition for the longer experience – where the theatrical encounter resonates in the minds, bodies and memories of its audience – is primarily motivated by a sense that this enhances the intrinsic experience of theatre as theatre. And moreover, that without this intrinsic reward none of the potential instrumental returns happen anyway. Finally, and more ideologically, it is shaped by a sense that the transfixed gaze of the audience, the unthinking, unblinking eye of passive consumption can only be countered by ensuring that spectators are actively processing and evaluating their experiences and as a result become cultural producers of meaning.

References

Adams, E. (2002), 'Power Drawing', *International Journal of Art and Design Education*, 21: 3, pp. 220–33.

Apter, K. (2009), 'Dance Review: Echoa', *The Scotsman*, 1 June, www.news.scotsman.com/reviews/Dance-review-Echoa.5322021.jp (accessed 28 February 2013).

Barba, E. (1990), 'Four Spectators', *The Drama Review*, 34, pp. 96–100.

Barker, M. (2006), 'I Have Seen the Future and It is Not Here Yet … Or, on Being Ambitious for Audience Research', *The Communication Review*, 9, pp. 123–41.

Bennett, S. (1997), *Theatre Audiences: A Theory of Production and Reception*, London: Routledge.

Eynon, K., 'Arcosm Company, Echoa', Londondance.com, www.londondance.com/reviews_details.asp?C=Arcosm+Company&P=Echoa&V=Millfield+Arts+Centre/ (accessed June 2010).

Feldman, E. B. (1995), *Verities of Visual Experiences*, New York: H. N. Abrams.

Gardner, L. (2002), 'The Quality of Children's Theatre', Birmingham: Arts Council of England.

Greene, M. (1995), *Releasing the Imagination: Essays on Education, the Arts, and Social Change*, San Francisco: Jossey-Bass.

Johanson, K. & Glow, H. (2011), 'Being and Becoming: Children as Audiences', *New Theatre Quarterly* 27: 1, pp. 60–70.

Klein, J. (2005), 'From Children's Perspective: A Model of Aesthetic Processing in Theatre', *Journal of Aesthetic Education*, 39: 4, pp. 40–57.

McGrath, A. (2010), 'Introduction', *Evaluating the Performing Arts: A Step by Step Teaching Guide*, Edinburgh: Imaginate.

McMaster, B. (2008), 'Supporting Excellence in the Arts: From Measurement to Judgement', London: Department for Culture, Media and Sport.

Reason, M. (2008), 'Thinking Theatre: Enhancing Children's Theatrical Experiences Through Philosophical Enquiry', *Philosophy and Childhood*, www.filoeduc.org/childphilo/n7/Matthew_Reason.pdf. (accessed 11 November 2011).

Reason, M. (2010), *The Young Audience: Exploring and Enhancing Children's Experiences of Theatre*, Stoke on Trent: Trentham.

Reason, M. and Reynolds, D. (2010), 'Kinesthesia, Empathy, and Related Pleasures: An Inquiry in Audience Experiences of Watching Dance', *Dance Research Journal*, 42: 2, pp. 49–75.

Sauter, W. (2003), 'Who Reacts When, How and upon What: From Audiences Surveys to the Theatrical Event', *Contemporary Theatre Review*, 12: 3, pp. 115–29.

Schonmann, S. (2006), *Theatre as a Medium for Children and Young People: Images and observations*, Dordrecht: Springer.

Taunton, M. (1983), 'Questioning Strategies to Encourage Young Children to Talk about Art', *Art Education*, 36: 4, pp. 40–43.

Chapter 8

Innovative Methods of Inquiry into Arts Engagement

Lisa Baxter, Daragh O'Reilly and Elizabeth Carnegie

Recent years have seen a welcome growth in the innovative use of research methods in arts marketing scholarship. The call for publications for the special issue of the *International Journal of Culture, Tourism and Hospitality Research* (Larsen and O'Reilly 2010) was a deliberate attempt to address the relative lack of variety in methods, which had tended to be limited to questionnaire surveys and semi-structured interviews. This is not to decry the latter, of course, more a question of seeking alternative insights through other lenses and approaches, particularly qualitative (see Baxter 2010). After all, arts consumption experiences are complex (Lee et al. 1994; Parry and Johnson 2007). The overall goal is to improve the theoretical understanding of arts marketing and consumption practices. One way to do this is to open the door to methods that have been used in other areas but not yet applied within the arts. The special issue mentioned above included papers on conversation analysis (O'Sullivan 2010), video studies (Vom Lehn 2010), personal construct psychology (Slater 2010), introspection (Patterson 2010) and grounded theory (Goulding and Saren 2010). None of these are radically innovative, in so far as, for example, personal construct psychology was originally formulated in 1955, grounded theory in 1967 and conversation analysis in the late 1960s. However, their application to arts marketing is a new departure, and one that has shown promise of new and useful insights.

Academic-practitioner cooperation

In 2008–2009, the authors worked together on a project funded by the UK Arts and Humanities Research Council (AHRC) and Arts Council England (ACE), which brought both arts marketing scholars and practitioners together in a series of workshops to discuss innovation in research methods. The workshop process clearly illustrated differences in the ways in which scholars and practitioners think about the arts experience and research methods. The challenge was to develop an experimental, innovative inquiry design that would seek to surface rich consumer insights into arts engagement and consumption. The project included the opportunity to trial new methods with arts and leisure audiences, specifically customers of the West Yorkshire Playhouse, Leeds – a major regional producing theatre – and Magna Science Adventure Centre – a £46 million Millennium Commission Lottery-funded project in Rotherham. The methods chosen for working with the audience members and visitors included the use of *graphic ideation* (see Bagnoli 2009; Banks 1998), *timelines,* and *metaphor elicitation.* Since the conclusion of the project, one of the authors (Baxter) has used and developed these methods extensively in her professional arts research consultancy practice. This chapter reports on how this has been carried out.

Commercial pressures

Generally speaking, research methods' innovation and scholarship in the arts are removed from the pressures of the commercial practices of arts marketing research. Theatres, galleries, museums and arts development agencies often depend on these arts research practitioners for their customer insights. Just like their commercial counterparts, arts organizations do not have in-house market research resources, and so have to commission studies externally. An arts marketing researcher who earns his/her living from research has far less time to engage in leisurely examinations of behavioural phenomena. The research practitioner has to identify potential clients, bid for assignments in competition with others, select appropriate methods, gather data to help answer (often difficult) questions and provide valuable insights for clients into a wide range of strategic and tactical issues. Their personal reputation is on the line and the time available is limited. There is no peer review to act as a filter before publication, only a final presentation and report direct to the client.

Yet the perspective of the contracting researcher is rarely acknowledged in arts marketing scholarship. It is all very well to talk about the application of innovative methods in a journal article, but what kinds of innovation might be possible under commercial time pressures? If necessity becomes the mother of invention, what kinds of inventive or innovative research practice does it produce? This chapter aims to provide some answers. After a discussion of qualitative research consultancy in the arts, it focuses on case studies from the research practice of Lisa Baxter, founder of The Experience Business, to show how a range of relatively innovative methods were used. These cases include the BALTIC Centre for Contemporary Art in Gateshead, Lyric Hammersmith, Watford Palace Theatre and The Brindley Arts Centre in Runcorn, Cheshire.

Qualitative insight

Much research into arts consumption is still about the drivers behind purchase behaviour and about consumer attitudes. However, there has been an emerging trend for the use of more qualitative methods, and, within that, for greater innovation in the design of qualitative inquiries. The AHRC/ACE-funded project mentioned above has proved to be a significant catalyst in this area. In general, qualitative research consultancy in the area of arts marketing acts as an interface between the audience and the arts organization by exploring consumers' needs and aspirations, their personal, cultural and social contexts, their arts experiences and impacts, and their ideas and creativity. This type of consultancy could be said to be trying to awaken arts organizations so that they can fully appreciate the experiences and impacts of the work they are creating and managing. It also works with audiences and communities as creative resources for developing ideas and solutions to organizational challenges. The goal is to enable arts organizations to develop empathy with their audiences and communities, communicate persuasively to them, engage meaningfully with them, and shape resonant and relevant arts experiences and programmes with them and for them. This practice covers the area of branding, marketing and communications, audience development and engagement, visitor experience design and management, and finally organizational development.

For arts organizations operating in an experience economy, it is important to understand how they can deliver value through understanding the experiences they create and manage. It is not enough to count 'bums on seats'. They need to know and understand the ways in which the arts experiences they offer hold value for their audiences, and what kind of value that is, whether it be a good night out or a meaningful aesthetic experience. They need to access richer, deeper insights, to be more customer-focused and to make strong artistic and business decisions. There is also an increasing pressure to prove benefit to funders, who are demanding a more sophisticated understanding of the impact of their investment. The arts are increasingly under threat from other leisure and cultural pursuits that offer competing experiences. Arguably, arts organizations need to use insight to put the audience at the centre of their creative and professional practices.

In order to gain a deep insight into customers, it is necessary to use methods that are intuitive and immersive. The problem is that the arts consumption experience is complex, rich, multi-dimensional and hard to capture. What one captures depends on where one thinks the arts experience begins and ends, and whether one is looking at immediate intrinsic impacts or the lasting, cumulative impacts.

The key is not so much to 'do audience research' but instead for the consultant to do creative facilitation. This means s/he works with audiences as co-creators of ideas and solutions, not just the subjects of research. This involves working with arts organizations in a facilitative capacity, the role being to tap into the ideas and creative potential of audiences, work with them as co-authors of insight and the creators of user-generated solutions. It is creative, inspirational and exploratory, an empowering experience for participants, and enables them to see directly how their contribution has influenced the finished product. It also gives the client confidence to make informed decisions about meaningful audience engagement.

Research methods

This section considers metaphor, guided visualization and timeline work in the context of qualitative inquiry.

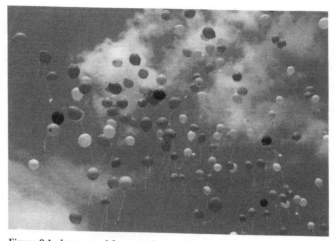

Figure 8.1: Image used for metaphor work. (Photo: Visual Explorer: Center for Creative Leadership).

Metaphor

Metaphors are a way of communicating rich meaning. They encourage respondents into right-brain thinking, which is more lateral and intuitive. When one probes the metaphor elicited from the informant, rich data emerges. A random selection of objects or images is placed on a table. Research participants are then invited to select one that for them connects with a particular question, for example, 'select an image which for you represents your best friend.' The chosen image then acts as a stimulus for dialogue. It is not the literal image that matters but the interpretation that is attached to it. Within a group context, this formed the basis of an exploration into shared meaning around the organization or experience in question. Figure 8.1 shows one of the images used for metaphor work.

Guided visualization

Guided visualization is used because it is a good way of immersing people in a specific arts experience(s). It can also guard against some of the imperfections of conscious memory. It is an evocative technique that guides participants to a different state of mind. It is not about remembering so much as the participant re-immersing himself or herself in the experience. It is a calm and quiet environment, and the trust of those with you is needed. The participants are taken on a guided 'journey' of about 15–20 minutes with the researcher using specific word prompts to attune participants to the sensory, emotional, and other intangible elements of experience. This encourages them to re-experience a specific arts event in the richest possible way. When the visualization is over, they are invited to draw

Figure 8.2: Drawing after guided visualization.
(Photo: Lisa Baxter, by kind permission of BALTIC
Centre for Contemporary Art).

whatever comes into their minds. The drawings provide immediate impressions of the visualization, and then act as an aid when discussing the experiences that were evoked. The drawings – like the metaphor cards – are not analysed by the researcher. It is the participants who bring their own meaning to the images. In this way, participants co-author the insights. Figure 8.2 shows an example of a drawing produced after a guided visualization.

Timelines

A timeline process can be used to help understand the roots of respondents'/participants' attitudes, values and motivational triggers. This provides valuable context when exploring experiences, the impacts of the arts and the subsequent value attached to them. Timeline drawing is a reflective exercise in which participants are invited to simply draw a line across a landscape-format piece of paper, to draw and reflect upon any significant milestones in their life in relation to their arts experiences, and then to relate them to their personal values. Figure 8.3 below illustrates a timeline produced by a participant.

The above methods, and others, were used as part of a creative facilitation approach in a number of commercially commissioned arts research projects. Highlights of these cases are presented in the following pages.

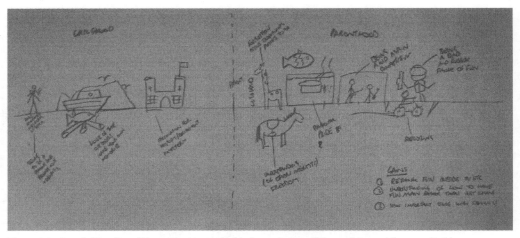

Figure 8.3: Sample Timeline. (Photo: Lisa Baxter, by kind permission of Magna Science Adventure Park).

BALTIC

BALTIC Centre for Contemporary Art ('BALTIC') is a major international arts organization. It was founded with funding from the UK National Lottery, the local council, the European Regional Development Fund and Arts Council England, among others. BALTIC is located in Gateshead in the north-east of England and opened in July 2002, attracting 35,000 visitors in the first week. It currently has a staff and crew of around 100 people. BALTIC has no collection of its own, but hosts a wide range of art exhibitions, including work by well-known figures such as Hirst, Kiefer and Ono. It hosted the prestigious and often controversial Turner Prize in 2011.

As part of its mission, BALTIC wanted to engage young people (who had no previous experience of it) in contemporary art. A group of 11–15 year olds who had never visited BALTIC before were invited to take part in creative workshops with artists to explore the work of Anselm Kiefer. The researcher's role was to act as a creative facilitator, to explore their expectations and experiences of BALTIC, develop new ideas for BALTIC's experience offering for 11–15 year olds and find new and interesting ways for BALTIC to communicate with young people.

The workshop was designed to research a number of areas: to explore participants' expectations of the project prior to commencement; to gain feedback on their experience of the building and its contents; to identify 'milestone' moments during their involvement in the project; to provide constructive feedback on how their experience was managed through the project; and to obtain experience and impact evidence to inform future visitor engagement initiatives. This two-hour session utilized a number of elicitation and projective techniques to encourage participants into a creative and generative mindset. The group was able to bring to awareness deeper insights than is usually possible through predominantly discussion-based approaches. The specific techniques employed included reflection – individual written work to minimize the risk of peer pressure and 'group think'; visual mapping of feedback to further stimulate discussion; post-it downloads to encourage continued thinking and avoid giving up after the first 'top-of-mind' answers; metaphor cards to stimulate richer thinking and generate intuitive insights; opportunities for participants' to draw their own conclusions from the discussions.

From this process, a range of fruitful findings emerged. It became clear that the participants felt a need to belong, to feel welcome, to 'own' some of BALTIC's outputs and to 'inhabit' the building. This could be described as 'claiming a physical and mental territory' within the building. They also felt a need to experiment and express themselves freely, to experiment with their self-expression and identity construction. There was the need to find an alternative – to a degree – to the controlling and possibly limiting influences of home and of institutions such as school. Finally, they needed to feel valued and important.

Participants' positive experiences at BALTIC can be broadly summarized as:

- Social – meeting new people and making new friends, either other participants or BALTIC staff and artists;
- Personal – developing confidence in themselves and their creative abilities;
- Creative – working with new materials and making art in interesting and new ways;
- Unexpected – the people they met, they ways in which they worked, the degree of enjoyment they derived and the ways in which they began to 'get' the art were all unexpected – in this respect, the project exceeded their expectations;
- Stretching – the project provided them with experiences that were new, different, unusual and exciting, described as an 'adventure'; and finally,
- The building – participants' experience of the building was a significant factor. They were impressed by the architecture, the views, the exhibitions, the fact there was a library, computer space and the Quay Space, and the retail/catering offer.

There were some negative experiences, too. The biggest theme that emerged was a sense of alienation or not belonging because some did not 'get' the art, the food and merchandise were unaffordable and the reception area was too formal.

The creative workshop also identified potential 'ingredients' for a successful youth engagement initiative. These are a social dimension, an element of experimentation and adventure, demystification and involvement with staff.

Lyric Online

Lyric Hammersmith, London, is a producing theatre that aims to 'produce work that is provoking, entertaining, popular, eclectic, messy, contradictory and diverse'. It wants to be at the heart of its community as well as being internationally recognized. It employs around

85 people. It was founded in 1895 as a small opera house. After closing in the 1960s, it was rebuilt in 1979 and redeveloped further in 2004. It currently presents around 1,000 performances and entertains over 150,000 people per year. Its current listings show a broad programming mix, including Edward Bond's *Saved*, a Christmas pantomime *Aladdin, A Midsummer Night's Dream* and *Lovesong* by Frantic Assembly.

Lyric wished to review its website in order to enhance its practical, strategic and brand functions. The research was commissioned to inform the website brief and designed to deliver insights that could help to shape technical and design specifications, positioning and potential engagement opportunities. The target group for the research was young people selected from the Lyric Young Company (for 11–25 year olds). The research was designed to explore their relationship with and perceptions of the Lyric and how it fitted into their lives, explore their online world and how they engage with the Internet, assess the degree of need to engage online with the Lyric beyond ticket purchase and, where appropriate, seek to identify suitable online engagement and communication vehicles.

Each participant was set a pre-task to 'warm them up' to the subject of enquiry beforehand, minimizing knee-jerk reactions and eliciting deeper insights during the allotted time. This pre-task invited participants to evaluate the Lyric's website beforehand. Participants were invited to select a number of picture cards that best represent the Lyric and themselves in order to reveal personal metaphors that get to the heart of their relationship with the venue

Figure 8.4: Mind-map from Lyric Online project.

and set the tone for the rest of the group discussion. This was followed by structured group discussions. Participants were asked to develop mind-maps for sharing within a group context. As with visual metaphor, this avoids automatic and cliché responses. Figure 8.4 shows a mind-map that emerged from this inquiry.

The research found that the Lyric occupied a central place in the lives of Lyric Young Company (LYC) members. It was perceived as a positive space, a 'family' and support network, a place where they felt equal, a place of opportunity and personal growth, a motivational and inspirational force and a significant turning point in their lives. LYC members were highly engaged, savvy Internet users. The Internet fulfilled a number of roles in their lives: functional (information, shopping), recreational (games, listening to music, media/TV downloads), social (primarily networking via Facebook) and personal (shaping and expressing their identity through cultural consumption and creative expression). LYC members also engaged with arts websites for access to cheap tickets, information and reviews, professional development and career opportunities.

The research revealed that LYC members were committed social networkers as well as enthusiastic Lyric advocates, and yet they 'rejected' the website. This led to the idea that aligning the site to their needs and affording them the status, presence, content, and modes of engagement they wanted (and in doing so, the validation they believed they deserved), the website could become a valuable advocacy tool with the potential to meaningfully engage with a broader circle of young people and potential audiences/participants.

Another finding was that the website did not at that time reflect 'their Lyric'. Over and above the shows, these research participants had a number of different brand or experience touch-points that, for them, meant 'Lyric' – from an 'edgy contemporary theatre' to a relaxing 'third space', a family friendly venue, a community hub, and a place where young people could really engage. The client needed to find ways of evoking and communicating 'Lyric-ness' through design, functionality, modes of engagement and strategic messaging. This raised issues about the control of Lyric's online identity. By 'letting go' a little, Lyric could help LYC members to feel more valued, motivated and empowered – in charge of a more convincing and persuasive advocacy tool that could draw more young people in to the Lyric.

Watford Palace Theatre

Watford Palace Theatre (WPT), is located in Hertfordshire, north of London. WPT produces high quality work that is distinctive and ambitious, embracing varied styles and cultures of theatre. This work both attracts artists of stature to Watford and provides opportunities to nurture new and emerging artists. It delivers enjoyable, exhilarating and accessible productions on stage and beyond. Participation is central to Watford Palace Theatre, which delivers a comprehensive range of projects for people of all ages and backgrounds in Watford, Hertfordshire and the surrounding region, as well as providing a platform for local talent.

The brief for this research project was to gain a more in-depth perspective on participants' experiences of the Milestones project, a community play performed in November 2008. The aim was to inform a continuance strategy that might include the cultivation of project ambassadors and additional community projects. The research was designed to yield intuitive, qualitative insights through the use of visual metaphor and graphic ideation. Idea generation and co-creational idea development were employed to generate a sense of ownership of the recommendations that flowed out from the discussions. A secondary aim of this particular combination of methods was to make the research session as creative, enjoyable and interactive as possible, thus acting as a valuable 'experience-point' that communicates the innate creativity of WPT. Image cards were employed to elicit insights into participants' perceptions of WPT. The cards were laid out on a table and participants were invited to choose ones that represented how they felt about or perceived WPT prior to their involvement in Milestones. The discussion then moved onto how those feelings and perceptions had changed through their experience of the project. Participants were then invited to create a drawing that represented their touch-points and subsequent turning points (or 'personal milestones') through the duration of the project. The exercise was not designed to create self-explanatory visual representations that could be interpreted as a

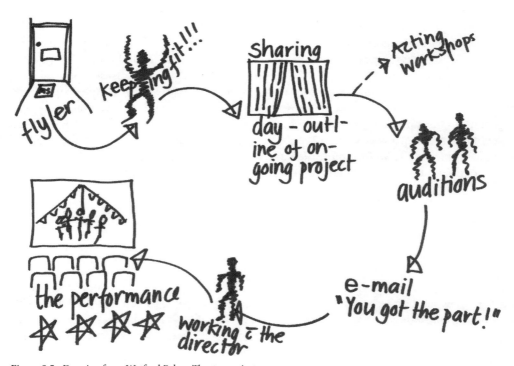

Figure 8.5: Drawing from Watford Palace Theatre project.

data source in itself, but employed as a means of 'tuning in' participants to the truth of their experience through silent, creative reflection. Some of the drawings created by the participants were eloquent storyboards that clearly articulated some of their personal milestones during the project. Figure 8.5 shows one of the drawings.

When analysing the conversations, it was hard to distinguish clearly between 'experiences' and 'impacts' because, in many cases, the experiences themselves were profoundly impactful, owing to their strength and depth. Looking at it from the perspective of impacts as 'take-aways', the key enduring personal impacts are the creation of a valued community of friends, a diminished sense of isolation or marginalization, a genuine identification with and appreciation of WPT, the relocation of WPT to a more central position in their lives, altered self-perceptions in relation to newly acquired skills, personal and social achievements and newly discovered talent and creativity.

The Brindley

The Brindley Arts Centre, based in Runcorn, Cheshire, is a purpose-built arts centre that opened in Halton in 2004. It is the only venue in Halton to offer high quality contemporary theatre work in a purpose-built environment. *Theatre for All* (2010–2012) is an audience development initiative, working together with partner theatre companies, designed to engage new audiences from the local community – particularly disadvantaged, hard-to-reach and vulnerable groups – in The Brindley's live programme, workshops and outreach work. The objectives of the *Theatre For All* project that relate to this qualitative evaluation are, among others: to identify and dismantle perceptual barriers to arts engagement; to offer a rewarding, positive, enjoyable experience through engaging with The Brindley; and to employ appropriate methods of engagement that meet the specific lifestyle, access and personal needs of each target group.

The researcher designed a programme of supportive evaluation aimed at providing qualitative insights on a project-by-project basis through consultation with the artistic project partners and participants. The focus of this particular discussion was the impact on, and journeys of, participants in a community choir that was created to take part in LipService Theatre Company's *Desperate to Be Doris* at The Brindley. *Desperate to Be Doris* was a piece of comedy musical theatre that was performed at a number of venues, each one involving a community choir. The Brindley's relationship with LipService has existed for several years. This show marked a new way for the two to work together creatively. The production was an ambitious project for LipService, which took it beyond its usual scale of operation. *Desperate to be Doris* was an opportunity for The Brindley to strengthen its community links through participatory activity. The aim was to generate a sense of local ownership of the project and produce a choir for The Brindley as a project legacy. In support of this, the venue funded the choir leader position and provided rehearsal space for the choir. From the perspective of LipService, this project was significant in developing the 'nature of engagement' with

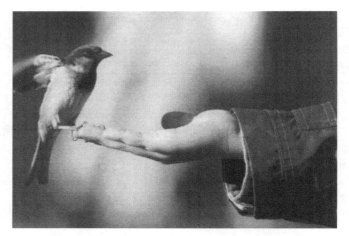

Figure 8.6: Metaphor card example from The Brindley Theatre Project. (Photo: Visual Explorer: Center for Creative Leadership).
'The Brindley is the hand and we are the bird. Suddenly we can fly off and do something great.'

partner venues and audiences, leading to their hope that the project would strengthen and progress their creative relationship with The Brindley.

Key methods used in this case were metaphor/image cards and group discussions. Figure 8.6 is an example of a metaphor card and participant quote. Participants perceived The Brindley, prior to their involvement in the project, as a place that 'brings people together'. The Brindley fulfils a number of different functions: a place to have fun, experience art and entertainment, a place to take part in a variety of activities (some participants were members of the a singing group) and a place to meet and socialize with friends.

Participants within the discussion group learned about the project through the singing group, or through publicity in the local newspaper. All attended a local taster event, enjoyed singing Doris Day songs at that event and were subsequently drawn into the project. When participants were asked about the impacts of being involved in the project, perhaps the biggest impact was that participants derived a huge amount of personal satisfaction, fulfilment and achievement from taking part in the choir. It offered them a break from the routine of their normal lives, provided an opportunity to express a different side of themselves and made them feel self-important, outside of the needs of their family. Their choir experience was precious and personal, which generated what one participant described as an 'inner glow'. The result was a genuine sense of self-actualization and a positively different sense of self after years of prioritizing their family. The choir leader added how she had witnessed members of the choir coming out of their shells and 'blossoming'.

All participants were asked to select metaphor cards that demonstrated 'their Brindley' after the project ended. In all cases, the images chosen represented a point of connection with The Brindley and its impact on them through the project. The Brindley was perceived as an enabler, a place of opportunity, a venue that brought the community together and a place where people could develop their potential. All these positive associations link in very closely to their experience of *Desperate to be Doris*.

Conclusion

This chapter has discussed several research methods not commonly used in academic arts marketing research and shown how they can help to generate useful insights for the strategic and tactical purposes of arts organizations. In addition to thinking of such inquiries as 'market research', we suggest that it can also be helpful to think of them as creative facilitations. This repositions research participants as active partners and not simply data sources. This involves re-imagining the relationship with the audience and giving them a voice within arts organizations. It is not about displacing the role of the artists or about 'dumbing down' the art. It is about the creation of people-focused enrichment strategies. It is also about being an explorer and adventurer; through qualitative consultancy and creative facilitation, one can explore uncharted territory and reveal new insights. It is possible to employ creative techniques that bring arts organizations and the public together to collaborate, inspire and challenge. In this way, one can identify and develop shared purpose and values between arts organizations and their publics.

References

Bagnoli, A. (2009), 'Beyond the Standard Interview: The Use of Graphic Elicitation and Arts-based Methods', *Qualitative Research*, 9: 5, pp. 547–570.

Banks, M. (1998), 'Visual Anthropology: Image, Object and Interpretation', in J. Prosser (ed.), *Image-based Research: A Sourcebook for Qualitative Researchers*, London: Falmer Press.

Baxter, L. (2010), 'Qualitative Research and the Arts: From Luxury to Necessity', in D. O'Reilly and F. Kerrigan (eds), *Marketing the Arts: A Fresh Approach*, London: Routledge.

Goulding, C. & Saren, M. (2010) 'Immersion, Emergence and Reflexivity: Grounded Theory and Aesthetic Consumption', *International Journal of Culture, Tourism and Hospitality Research*, 4: 1, pp. 70–82.

Larsen, G. & O'Reilly, D. (ed.) (2010), Special issue on creative methods of inquiry in arts marketing, *International Journal of Culture, Tourism and Hospitality Research*, 4: 1, pp. 3–7.

Lee, Y., Dattilo, J. & Howard, D. (1994), 'The Complex and Dynamic Nature of Leisure Experience', *Journal of Leisure Research*, 26: 3, pp. 195–211.

O'Sullivan, T. (2010), 'More than Words? Conversation Analysis in Arts Marketing Research', *International Journal of Culture, Tourism and Hospitality Research*, 4: 1, pp. 20–32.

Parry, D. C. & Johnson, C. W. (2007), 'Contextualizing Leisure Research to Encompass Complexity in Lived Leisure Experience: The Need for Creative Analytic Practice', *Leisure Sciences*, 29: 2, pp. 119–130.

Patterson, A. (2010), 'Art, Ideology, and Introspection', *International Journal of Culture, Tourism and Hospitality Research,* 4: 1, pp. 57–69.

Slater, A. (2010), 'Understanding Individual Membership at Heritage Sites', *International Journal of Culture, Tourism and Hospitality Research,* 4: 1, pp. 44–56.

Vom Lehn, D. (2010), 'Examining "Response": Video-based Studies in Museums and Galleries', *International Journal of Culture, Tourism and Hospitality Research,* 4: 1, pp. 33–43.

Chapter 9

Structure and Aesthetics in Audience Responses to Dance

Kim Vincs

P opular television shows such as *So You Think You Can Dance* celebrate the premise that responses to dance are highly subjective. The drama of the show is generated by the tension between the expert judges' opinions and those of the voting public, which sometimes agree and sometimes differ wildly. If this view is correct, then quality is in the eye of the beholder. This chapter examines new work in dance reception that uses real-time continuous measurement of audience response to examine the consistency or diversity of responses between audience members, and whether specific choreographic structures can be identified that tend to enhance an audience's engagement with the work. The results of these experiments suggest that audiences display higher levels of agreement in their responses to dance than might be expected, given the highly subjective nature of dance communication, and are to some extent responsive to choreographic phrasing in the sense of tension and release – increasing expectation and the fulfilment or delay of expectation.

Do they think you can dance?

The *So You Think You Can Dance* franchise (Fuller and Lythgoe 2005–2011) perfectly demonstrates the problem of audience response to dance performance. What is it that audiences respond to when they vote? What is it that the judges respond to when they critique the performances? Sometimes the judges disagree with each other, and sometimes the audience vote overturns the judges' opinions. What drives these wildly divergent responses? Is it the choreography, the technique, the 'performance quality', or simply the narrative packaging of the performers' lives, hopes and aspirations that forms the media framing of each performance and the drama of the competition?

Does dance scholarship, with its theoretical perspective informed by a generation of post-structuralist thought and by the artistic innovations of the steady stream of choreographers, beginning with Merce Cunningham in the 1950s, who have defined what we now know as contemporary dance, have anything to contribute to how mass television audiences respond to dance? By and large, the judges and audiences of dance reality TV shows haven't read contemporary performance studies, and even if they had, it is by no means clear what, if any, impact this body of theory would have on their responses to the dance performances before them.

A more fundamental question exists: is there any common conceptual basis on which audience responses to dance can be understood? This is a critical question for dance artists and companies, because although innovation and the creation of the new are a core artistic value, the economic survival and development of the work of artists and companies depends on the support of audiences. Innovation in art is a Darwinian process – if a particular kind of work does not draw an audience, economic reality will ensure it does not survive.

This chapter examines new research in dance reception that addresses this question by measuring audiences' levels of engagement with dances, to probe how consistent or diverse responses are between audience members, and whether any specific choreographic structures can be identified that enhance audiences' engagement with the work. The projects used portable palm-pilot devices on which audience members continuously recorded their levels of engagement, while viewing a series of dance performances. The responses were compared with a choreographic analysis of the dance and with motion-capture data of the kinematic dynamics of the movement. The results of these experiments show that audiences do display some agreement in their responses to dance, and that choreographic phrasing in the sense of tension and release – increasing expectation and the fulfilment or delay of expectation – has some bearing on these responses.

These outcomes suggest that dance reception might not be as subjective as has generally been assumed. This is a highly significant finding for dance artists and companies. If there are choreographic structures that can enhance engagement with a dance work based on common perceptual responses to dance movement, then understanding how these processes function is critical for dance artists and companies, both as a basis for creating dances that have the best possible chance of attracting audiences and as a provocative spur towards innovation.

Movement perception or cultural theory: Does movement matter?

A fundamental divide in audience research in dance is whether and how the fundamental processes of movement perception influence the reflective, post-performance interpretation of a dance work by audiences. A wave of new research into the neuroscience of dance has been sparked by technologies that offer the possibility of uncovering the underlying movement perception mechanisms that underpin dance reception. A number of recent studies have begun to measure and map the cortical activity that occurs while watching dance (Hagendoorn 2004; Calvo-Merino 2010; Brown et al. 2006; and Cross 2010). Calvo-Merino et al. (2009), for example, have demonstrated that previous visual and motor knowledge of dance experience enhances the perception of ballet movement and suggest that this effect involves configural action perception mechanisms in the brain. However, as Jola et al. (2011) point out, linking observers' subjective, phenomenological experiences with specific neurological mechanisms remains challenging as a result of the difficulty of testing holistic dance stimuli in real-world (theatre) conditions, and the methodological challenge of generalizing individual experiences to compare them with the statistical outcomes of scientific experiments.

Audience researchers such as Reason (2010) point out that audience response is not complete at the perceptual stage, while watching a dance work, but only constructed as an experience through post-performance reflection. In his words, '... an experience, therefore, is not just what is going on in an audience's mind (and body) during a performance, but also what they do with this experience after the event' (2010: 24). If this is the case, does movement perception have any real bearing on the experience of a dance work ultimately constructed by a viewer through ongoing processes of re-synthesizing and re-contextualizing the now-vanished moment of performance? Are the brain functions that perceive movement so overwritten by the reflective processes that occur after a performance as to be rendered largely irrelevant to the cultural/textural 'reading' of a work?

Post-structuralist dance scholarship would predict that this is indeed the case. When understood from the perspective Susan Melrose (2003) termed the 'textural turn' in dance scholarship, which emphasizes semiotic readings of dance works over the formal, material qualities of the work, dance movement is coded via multiple, complex, overlapping and not necessarily epistemologically coherent or temporally stable frames of reference. Even if the neuroscientific basis of movement perception could be unpacked in sufficient detail to account for dance reception, these processes may be so comprehensively overwritten by polyvalent culturally mediated processes of interpretation as to have no real impact on the artistic and cultural effect of dance on its audiences.

An alternative analysis of this question, however, can be provided by an examination of Laurence Louppe's description of the poetics of contemporary dance (Louppe 2010). Contemporary dance operates poetically and ontologically via movement. Contemporary dance is not simply a re-arrangement of dance elements into a novel 'style', but an instantiation, through movement, of a way of 'being in the world'. Susanne Langer's (1953) argument that dance creates a primary illusion of virtual force through which the agency of the dancer in the world is symbolically communicated, although based on a 1940s ontology of communication in which meaning maps more or less isomorphically to metaphor, anticipates Louppe's assertion that contemporary dance is not a decorative form, but fundamentally concerned with articulating subjectivity through movement.

That this articulation occurs through movement seems to state the obvious. However, the slippage between movement and text that is implicit in Melrose's 'textural turn' in dance research, whereby dance analysis can be considered a sub-branch of performance semiotics and therefore always reducible to language, makes it necessary to be clear about this distinction. While dance may be partially interpretable using textural analysis, the poetics of dance in fact lie within the organization of the body and its movement – an organization that takes place spatially, in the materiality of the relationship between body parts, and temporally, via the trajectories of the body in space/time, rather than through the mere naming of movement after the fact. Dance operates via a spatiotemporal logic, not a verbal one, to create an image of a person 'being in the world'. As Louppe describes it,

> action is the consciousness of a subject in the world ... The dancer, however, has no other support at her/his disposal than what shows and above all localises her/him as this subject in the world: a body and this body's movement created from an extreme

'nearness', without any other projection in an already instituted (verbal) code. The dancer has nothing exterior or supplementary to the matter/material of self with which to build a signifying universe, an intelligible imaginary.

(Louppe 2010: 23)

Post-performance evaluations have been the mainstay of audience research in dance because they provide an assessment of how audiences 'read' dance performances in a cultural sense. However, insofar as they are based on verbal methods (discussions and/or questionnaires and surveys), as in the work of Glass (2005), for example, they cannot provide information about the spatiotemporal nature of audiences' engagement with dance movement itself – in effect, the poetics of the art forms. Exceptions include work such as Reason's, which use non-verbal methods such as drawing to elicit post-performance responses (Reason 2010). However, even when the methodology of response is non-verbal, post-performance reflection still only taps an audience's reflective interpretation of a performance after the fact. The dynamics by which the organization of dancing bodies in space themselves embody the poetic of the form are not easily extractable from any method of post-performance evaluation. Real-time response evaluation, that is, recording audience responses to dance while they are watching, measures responses before the performance is finished and therefore before a complete 'experience' of the dance can be constructed. This method therefore offers a means of studying responses to the spatiotemporal dynamics of dance movement independently of their post-performance construction into a meaningful experience.

This method might, at first glance, seem to suffer from a lack of cultural and contextual engagement. However, it is possible to re-think, as many contemporary art and cognitive science researchers are now beginning to do, the relationship between brain and culture in a way that resolves this tension. Scott deLahunta (2004), for example, drawing on his extensive collaborations between choreographers and cognitive scientists, argues that brain research charts the mental spaces that underpin dance creation, which are instantiated in simultaneously structural and cultural terms. In his words, cognitive science charts '... dynamic systems of thought through references to abstract spaces and processes that are no less real than the brain' (deLahunta 2004: 1). Barbara Stafford (2007) argues that both culture and brain have been formed by the same evolutionary and societal forces. Knowledge generated by contemporary neuroscience about how the brain perceives and understands patterns in sensory input through art is therefore simply another way of understanding the cultural forces that shape us, because brain function and cultural influence exist in a mutual relationship in which each shapes the other. In her words, 'pattern formation and pattern recognition – from schematic outline to full-blown illusionism – illuminate both neural functions and symbolic processes resulting from social agency' (Stafford 2007: 11).

Brain function and cultural construction can be thought of as two sides of the same coin, rather than as a one-way process through which cultural semiotics re-code perceptual processes to create meaning. In dance reception, it is important to study movement itself and the underlying perceptual and cognitive processes through which we perceive it because dance articulates subjectivity in spatiotemporal terms. Dance 'speaks' by means of the perceptual mechanisms through which we apprehend movement as well as by semiotic translations of them. That dance perception is the basis for a larger construction – Reason's ongoing re-versioning of a dance as an 'experience' that occurs post-performance (which, as in the original example of *So You Think You Can Dance*, is always embedded in a myriad of wider social and media contexts) – does not mean that choreographic structure itself can be ignored as incidental to a verbal 'overwriting' of the experience of dance.

Measuring continuous responses to dance

In this section, I will draw on the combined results of a series of experiments in measuring continuous responses to dance that took place over three years as part of a collaboration between myself and cognitive scientists Professor Catherine Stevens, of MARCS Auditory Laboratories, University of Western Sydney, and Associate Professor Emery Schubert, from the School of Music and Music Education, University of New South Wales. While the results have been individually published elsewhere (Schubert et al. 2008 and in press; Vincs et al. 2009; Vincs et al. 2010), my purpose here is to situate this work, which suggests that audience responses to dance are influenced by the dynamic and temporal structures of the dance, as well as by the cultural contexts and interpretations that arise from the movement, within the context of contemporary dance aesthetics, and to explore some of its implications for audience research in dance.

We measured the responses of contemporary dance students and experts to a range of dances, both student and professional, using a system of hand-held palm-pilot devices developed at MARCS Auditory Laboratories, called the 'pARF' system (Stevens et al. 2009). The dances and participants are summarized in Table 9.1. We asked our participants to record their continuous levels of engagement with the dance works as they watched by moving a stylus horizontally across the hand-held devices on a scale of 0–10, where 0 was completely unengaged and 10 was completely engaged, with engagement defined as being

> compelled, drawn in, connected to what is happening, interested in what will happen next. This term is often used by choreography teachers because it implicitly directs students towards evaluating a dance's ability to employ structural logic and movement imagery to draw an audience's attention, rather than towards its ability to 'entertain' (although the two are not mutually exclusive).
>
> (Vincs et al. 2009: 3)

Rather than pre-empting the structure of their responses, we provided no information to our observers about what might constitute a change of engagement. We wanted to allow the participants to decide whether their experience of engagement was based on individual movements or on more extended temporal states of 'engagement'. The participants' responses

Table 9.1: Summary of Stimuli and Participants

Experiment	Stimulus		Observers
1	Semi-improvised physical theatre work by emerging artist	12 minutes	Ten second-year dance students Two dance experts
2	Three second-year dance student choreographic studies One PhD dance work in progress	1.5–3 minutes 3 minutes	Seven second-year dance students Four dance experts
3	Solo work by professional contemporary dance artist	6 minutes	Twelve dance students Seven dance experts

were synchronized and sampled by a central server twice every second. We then plotted the average engagement over time across all the observers.

Given the complexity of choreographic structures, in which different organizational schemas can be in play across different regions of the body at the same time, and in which the organizational basis for movement can change from moment to moment (e.g., initiation of sequential movement through the body, movement that is directed towards achieving a specific shape in space, movement that achieves locomotion, etc.), we did not attempt to predict or separate specific kinds of movement for response. Instead, we looked at moments when the average engagement of the group of observers rose more suddenly, and then analysed the video and (in the case of the third experiment) motion-capture recording of the dance to see what kinds of chorographic events were taking place when average engagement rose. In order to eliminate minor fluctuations, we chose only those moments when more quickly increasing engagement was followed by periods of sustained increasing engagement.

In looking at average engagement, we were asking what kinds of choreographic structures might enhance the engagement of any or all of our observers. That is to say, average engagement can rise because most observers record a rise in their engagement, or because a few observers, or even a single observer, records a strong rise in engagement while other observers record no rise, or even a decrease in their engagement. The point here is therefore not to definitively determine that some choreographic structures engage all observers, but to begin to understand what kinds of structures are capable of engaging some or any observers. We looked at the degree of agreement between observers using the standard deviation across the responses and Schubert's detailed analysis of agreement between individual observers revealed a complex picture of consensus and disagreement (Schubert et al. 2009 and in press).

We termed, perhaps provocatively, the moments in the dance when average engagement rose, 'gem moments' (Vincs et al. 2007 and 2009). The surprising finding was that although the dances we tested were quite disparate in movement aesthetic and in the experience and expertise of the artists, the responses to all the works showed increases in average engagement following similar kinds of choreographic phrasing and structure. Specifically, virtually all the 'gem moments' seemed to be associated with changes in dynamic and/or expectation in the dances. However, the converse was not true – not all changes in dynamic or expectation were associated with increased engagement, indicating that positioning within dance's overall sequencing and structure is also important.

The movement structures associated with 'gem moments' were differently constituted within the aesthetic and movement organization of each dance. In the physical theatre work, 'gem moments' were associated with sudden disjunctures of form and style. For example, quirky, unexpected hand gestures interspersed with more fluid, technical dancing were associated with a sudden increase in average engagement, as were sudden changes in intention, such as a transition to speaking, and the build up to a verbal joke. The student choreographic studies, in contrast, were based on movement invention and phrasing, and focused on formal movement manipulation rather than narrative. However, 'gem moment' responses in the student studies were, like those in the physical theatre work, associated with shifts in expectation. In these works, shifts in expectation tended to be generated by sudden dynamic shifts in the movement – moments when a movement phrase was suddenly interrupted or shifted dynamically. Interruptions often involved sudden, sharp or fast movements, or the addition of a small accented detail to the base movement.

The excerpt from the PhD work in progress was stylistically similar to the choreographic studies. The movement in this work was, for the most part, very slow, punctuated at unexpected moments by tiny, fleeting dynamic accents – for example, a sudden burst of energy took the performer's fingers apart by a few inches, and a sudden tension filled his body as he raised his head from the floor. Despite the significant differential in experience and complexity, the dynamic shifts in the PhD study gave rise to 'gem moment' responses in much the same way as those of the student studies.

The six-minute dance by a professional choreographer/performer also elicited rises in engagement that were associated with sudden dynamic and contextual shifts in the movement. This work comprised complex movement in which the dancer layered many subtle shifts in gaze, physical intention and body shape into what could be thought of as a moving 'tapestry' of contrasting images. The dance was slow in tempo, with many short pauses, structured as several over-arching sections, each comprised of a slowly evolving minutiae of shifts in physical intention, each executed with precise changes in physical tension and dynamic.

The levels of agreement between the observers varied across the different dances. For the physical theatre work, for example, the average standard deviation was 2.03 to 3.76 points, or 18.5 per cent to 34 per cent of the scale, meaning that two-thirds of the participants agreed, at a minimum to within 34 per cent of the scale, and at best to 18.5 per cent of the scale (Schubert et al. in press). In the case of the professional dance (experiment 3), we were able to compare the responses of dance experts and students and found that dance experts responded with more frequent 'gem moments' – sudden increases in engagement – than dance students when watching the professional dance (Vincs et al. 2010). Also of note is that increasing

Absolute Acceleration Head, Pelvis, Hands, Feet Markers versus Time

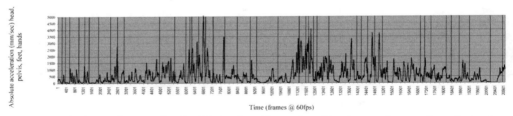

Figure 9.1: Absolute acceleration of head, pelvis, hands and feet markers. Six minute performance by professional dance artist, N = 19; 7 dance experts and 12 dance students. Vertical lines indicate gem moments by experts, students or both.

engagement was not necessarily associated with increasing agreement. Rather, increasing engagement actually tended to be associated with decreasing agreement between observers, and vice versa (Vincs et al. 2010). These levels of agreement indicate that while there is certainly considerable variation between observers, there is also significant agreement within the responses indicating that there seem to be common elements in the dances that influence average engagement.

In the third experiment, the professional choreographer's work was also motion-captured using a 24-camera Motion Analysis optical motion capture system so that the kinematics of specific movements could be compared with levels of observer engagement with the dance. Motion-capture data was used to calculate the absolute acceleration for top of head, pelvis (root), right and left finger and toe markers as a measure of the level of dynamic shift in six major body segments (head, trunk, R & L arms and legs). Summing the acceleration of the major extremities of the body provides an overview of the relative dynamic activity of the body at different points of the dance, rather than a fine-grained movement analysis. This technique provides a 'semantically blind' (Vincs 2011) appraisal of the overall level of dynamic activity in a movement sequence, although any meaning arising from the sequential ordering of this movement will be lost to this analysis. Figure 9.1 shows that many rises in engagement are associated with increasing or decreasing dynamic – either acceleration or deceleration – although, as would be expected given that choreographic disjuncture can be created by a number of different means, not all rises in engagement are attributable to dynamic change in the movement.

Audience response and contemporary dance aesthetics

It is difficult to underestimate the impact of Merce Cunningham's displacement of the effect of the body on contemporary dance. His work rejected the projection of desire as the goal of contemporary dance and replaced expressivity with an appreciation of 'presence' embodied by movement. This intervention was accomplished in no small part by Cunningham's complete revision of the idea of time in dance. Rather than the vector of desire and agency, Cunningham viewed time as a container for movement – something perceptible in and of itself, as duration, rather than as a means of communicating specific human intention (Louppe 2010). Where the early modern dancers, such as Wigman and Graham, made work that used tension and release to foreground the release of affect through time, for Cunningham,

> [t]he structure, the 'counts' can be perceived in the ongoing movement as a time 'frame' that distributes the accents, but they are not always marked by a change of weight and even less by tonic changes in the body – which remains neutral. This is Cunningham's ongoing project (unfinished even today) – to eliminate affects and their corresponding tensions, not so much perhaps because of their referential character but because their spasmodics tend to make time itself unreadable.
>
> (Louppe 2010: 99–100)

Cunningham's interventions have now become embedded in mainstream contemporary dance to the point where it is no longer possible to differentiate purely 'objectivist' dance since the influence of this kind of work has been integrated into mainstream contemporary dance training (Dempster 1994–1995), as part of what Louppe (1996) describes as a hybridization of initially very different aesthetic dance practices. Cunningham's work initiated a rejection of phrasing itself as a primary symbolic form in dance that is perhaps most famously demonstrated by Yvonne Rainer's *Trio A* in which she refused all forms of dynamic 'punctuation' in dance and eliminated all dynamic build up (Banes 1980; Livet 1978). So effective has this intervention been that deLahunta (2005) could argue that phrasing is no longer even considered a valid part of dance creation by some artists, and was able to demonstrate that its interpretation is highly variable even among dance artists who do still consider it important.

If the cognitive 'mapping' of dance is aligned to the culturally prevalent dance aesthetics observers have been exposed to, given the post-Cunningham hybridization of choreographic practices, and given the move away from 'tension and release' as a normative compositional structure over the last 50 years, one would not expect to find observers' responses to dance to entrain strongly to dynamic phrasing in the dance. Our recording of increased engagement associated with choreographic disjuncture and surprise across a range of different dances suggests that responses to dance may remain more consistently influenced by choreographic phrasing, in the sense of periodically increasing and decreasing expectation and the fulfilment or delay of these expectations, or what Doris Humphrey (1987) called 'tension and release', than one might imagine given the challenges to this kind of choreographic organization that have been mounted by objectivist/formalist dance practices over the past 50 years.

That phrases structured via disjuncture and surprise were associated with increased engagement of some of our contemporary dance observers raises the question of the timeframe between the formation of brain processes of perception and shifts in dance aesthetics and meaning. It is perhaps reasonable to assume that while the two systems interact, they do not completely rewrite each other in real-time. Perceptual mechanisms formed in response to specific cultural contexts and dance aesthetics may be in play in forming responses to artwork that is conceived and created from entirely different contexts and assumptions. Perceptual elements of audience responses to dance that have their genesis in completely different historical contexts may become temporally displaced from the work to which they respond.

This would create a system in which dance response could potentially be based on a range of overlapping and not necessarily ontologically cohesive perceptual/cultural mechanisms, and their associated (and not necessarily fixed) semiotics. It is perhaps fair to say that dance reception presents a complex perceptual picture that leaves 'cognitively targeting' dances (to borrow Calvo-Merino's speculation on the possibility of 'neurotargeting' dance) some way from reality (Calvo-Merino et al. 2008: 918). However, ignoring the effect of the brain mechanisms of movement perception that underpin dance reception in favour of a completely semiotized model would seem to be equally dangerous. Perhaps a more intriguing question underpinning this debate is to what extent the perceptual mechanisms underlying dance movement reception are related to dance aesthetics per se and/or to older, more fundamental evolutionary forces such as the detection of change in the environment as signals of danger or opportunity. If it were possible to probe this nexus, a deeper, if not necessarily simple or easily translatable, basis for understanding the poetics of dance might be made possible.

Acknowledgements

I would like to acknowledge and thank my collaborators Kate Stevens and Emery Schubert, along with the dance artists who contributed their work to the project, the student and expert dance participants, and research assistants Katrina Rank, Thomas Salisbury, Daniel Skovli, Peter Divers, Johnson Chen, Phoebe Robinson and Kim Barbour. This research is supported by grants from the Australian Research Council Discovery Project (DP0987101) and Linkage Project (LP0562687) schemes, and dance industry partners The Australia Council for the Arts Dance Board, The Australian Dance Council – Ausdance, ACT Cultural Facilities Corporation, and QL2 Centre for Youth Dance (formerly The Australian Choreographic Centre).

References

Banes, S. (1980), *Terpischore in Sneakers: Post-Modern Dance*, Boston: Houghton Mifflin Company.
Brown, S., Martinez, M. & Parsons, L. (2006), 'The Neural Basis of Human Dance', *Cerebral Cortex* 16: 8, pp. 1157–1167.

Calvo-Merino, B. (2010), 'Neural Mechanisms for Seeing Dance', in B. Bläsing, M. Puttke & T. Shack (eds), *The Neurocognition of Dance*, London: Psychology Press, pp. 153–176.

Calvo-Merino, B., Jola, C., Glaser, D. & Haggard, P. (2008), 'Towards a Sensorimotor Aesthetics of Performing Art', *Consciousness and Cognition*, 17, pp. 911–922.

Calvo-Merino, B., Ehrenberg, S., Leung, D. & Haggard, P. (2009), 'The Experts See it All', *Psychological Research*, 74: 4, pp. 400–406.

Cross, E. (2010), 'Building a Dance in the Human Brain: Insights from Expert and Novice Dancers', in B. Bläsing, M. Puttke & T. Schack (eds), *The Neurocognition of Dance*, London: Psychology Press, pp. 177–202.

deLahunta, S. (2004), 'Separate Spaces: Some Cognitive Dimensions of Movement', in *Species of Spaces* (DIFFUSION ebook series), London: Proboscis, pp. 1–7, http://diffusion.org.uk/ (accessed 30 September 2011).

——— (2005), 'What's in a Phrase?', in J. Birringer & J. Fenger (eds), *Tanz im Kopf: Jarbuch 15 der Gesellschaft für Tanzforschung*, Munster: LIT Verlag, http://www.choreocog.net/texts/ phraseinpress2.pdf. (accessed 30 September 2011).

Fuller, S. & Lythgoe, N. (2005–2011), *So You Think You Can Dance*, TV programme, Fox Broadcasting Company.

Glass, Renee (2005), 'Observer Response to Contemporary Dance', in R. Grove, C. Stevens & S. McKechnie (eds), *Thinking in Four Dimensions: Creativity and Cognition in Contemporary Dance*, Melbourne: Melbourne University Press, pp. 107–120, http://books.google.com. au/books?hl=en&lr=&id=3a1q_o2_NE4C&oi=fnd&pg=PA107&dq=Renee+Glass&ots =xutHD_MNFL&sig=s6CjbFzDc6MVSsNr9QTNRykoAqA#v=onepage&q=Renee%20 Glass&f=false (accessed 30 September 2011).

Hagendoorn, I. (2004), 'Some Speculative Hypotheses about the Nature and Perception of Dance and Choreography', *Journal of Consciousness Studies*, 11: 3/4, pp. 79–110.

Humphrey, D. (1987), *The Art of Making Dances*, Princeton, NJ: Princeton Book Company.

Jola, C., Ehrenberg, S. & Reynolds, D. (2011), 'The Experience of Watching Dance: Phenomenological-Neuroscience Duets', *Phenomenology and the Cognitive Sciences*, DOI: 10.1007/s11097-010-9191-xOnline First™.

Langer, S. (1953), *Feeling and Form: A Theory of Art*, New York: Scribner.

Livet, A. (1978), *Contemporary Dance*, New York: Abbeville Press.

Louppe, L. (2010), *The Poetics of Contemporary Dance*, translated from French by S. Gardener, Hampshire: Dance Books Ltd.

Melrose, S. (2003), *The Curiosity of Writing (or, Who Cares about Performance Mastery?)*, http:// www.sfmelrose.u-net.com/curiosityofwriting/ (accessed 30 September 2011).

Reason, M. (2010), 'Asking the Audience: Audience Research and the Experience of Theatre', *About Performance* 10, pp. 15–34.

Schubert, E., Vincs, K. & Stevens, C. (2008), 'A Quantitative Approach to Analysing Reliability of Engagement Responses to Dance', *Proceedings of the World Dance Alliance Global Summit, Brisbane, July 14–16*, Ausdance National, http://www.ausdance.org.au/resources/publications/ dance-dialogues/papers/analysing-reliability-of-engagement-responses-to-dance.pdf. (accessed 30 September 2011).

——— (in press), 'Identifying Regions of Agreement Among Responders in Engagement with a Piece of Live Dance', *Empirical Studies of the Arts*.

Stafford, B. (2007), *Echo Objects: The Cognitive Work of Images*, London and Chicago: University of Chicago Press.

Stevens, C., Schubert, E., Morris, R., Frear, M., Chen, J., Healy, S., Schoknecht, C. & Hansen, S. (2009), 'Cognition and the Temporal Arts: Investigating Audience Response to Dance Using PDAs that Record Continuous Data During Live Performance', *International Journal of Human-Computer Studies*, 67: 9, pp. 800–813.

Vincs, K. (2011), 'Capturing Dance and Choreotopography: Analyzing and Visualizing Complexity', [conference presentation], *The 17th International Symposium on Electronic Art (ISEA), Istanbul*, 14–21 September.

Vincs, K., Schubert, E. & Stevens, C. (2007), 'Engagement and the "Gem" Moment: How Do Dance Students View and Respond to Dance in Real Time?' *Proceedings of the 17th Annual Meeting of the International Association for Dance Medicine & Science*, Canberra, Australia, pp. 230–233.

——— (2009), 'Measuring Responses to Dance: Is There a "Grammar" of Dance?' *Proceedings of the World Dance Alliance Global Summit, Brisbane, July 14–16, 2008*, Ausdance National, http://www.ausdance.org.au/resources/publications/dance-dialogues/papers/is-there-a-grammar-of-dance.pdf. (accessed 30 September 2011).

Vincs, K., Stevens, C. & Schubert, E. (2010), 'Effects of Observer Experience on Continuous Measures of Engagement with a Contemporary Dance Work', in W. Christensen, E. Schier & J. Sutton (eds), *ASCS09: Proceedings of the 9th Conference of the Australasian Society for Cognitive Science*, pp. 357–361, Sydney, Macquarie Centre for Cognitive Science. http://www.maccs.mq.edu.au/news/conferences/2009/ASCS2009/pdfs/Vincs.pdf (accessed 30 September 2011).

Chapter 10

Converging with Audiences

Jennifer Radbourne

The new theories and discourse in the creative industries have revealed a necessary relationship between producer and consumer, which, in the performing arts, is demonstrated by a recognizable change in the relationship between artist or performer and audience. Relationship marketing theory has been challenged by the new arts consumer who is on a quest for self-actualization where the creative or cultural experience is expected to fulfil a spiritual need that has very little to do with the traditional marketing plan of an arts company or organization. This chapter scans arts marketing developments over the past thirty years to arrive at an examination of authenticity that engages a new individualistic, independent, informed and involved arts consumer who is changing the marketing paradigm. Through examples of theatre and orchestral audiences, a new paradigm of convergence marketing is characterized, and a model for practice proposed.

Arts marketing – an organization and product focus

The first publications on arts marketing appeared in the late 1970s and early 1980s and focused on differentiating arts marketing from existing mainstream marketing literature. Most arts organizations had become comfortable with government or philanthropic sources of revenue, and were not skilled in marketing strategies. Product selection, whether the season's repertoire or calendar of events, was largely driven by an artistic director who focused on his or her own artistic skills with minimal understanding of the needs of the audience. The arts organizations engaged in mass communication and were product and sales oriented, focusing on satisfying the organization's needs rather than the needs of the customer (Scheff 2007:10–11). Artists and artistic directors feared sacrificing their artistic integrity if programming was customer oriented. As competition for earned revenue and for the expected external funding increased, attention turned to subscription selling and promotional strategies to achieve, primarily, the artistic mission, and secondly, a financial return (Diggles 1986). Gradually, attention was given to finding out what motivates arts consumers. By the 1990s organizations were engaging in market research to analyse the demographics of their customers, and use this to develop arts product, price, promotion and place strategies (Radbourne and Fraser 1996). Data was collected, audiences segmented and programmes developed to meet the requirements of this new audience information. However, this research lacked sophistication and did not include an understanding of the values and lifestyles of audiences, nor that the arts experience was critical in attracting audiences.

Relationship marketing in the arts

Increasingly non-profit arts organizations learned from their commercial counterparts that entrepreneurs and successful businesses utilize market research extensively. Their customer orientation required a regular study of customer needs and wants, perceptions and attitudes, preferences and satisfactions. New courses in arts marketing and commissioned reports on audiences created greater awareness for arts organizations around the concept of the intangibility of the arts experience. The organization was not selling tickets, but selling an experience. While the tangible product could be touched, seen or heard, and augmented by adding refreshments, a programme or information talk, parking, or even a guarantee, the intangible satisfaction of the customer's need was at the core of the arts product or event. The arts product was linked to lifestyle choice and values. Even when the arts product is tangible,

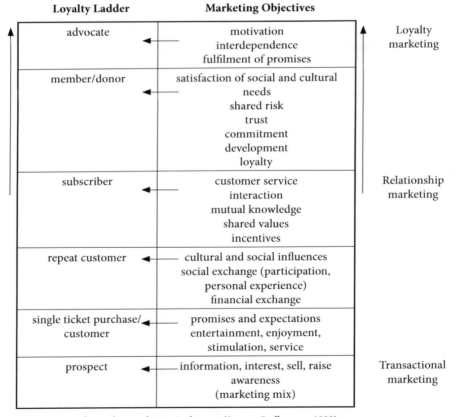

Figure 10.1: Relationship marketing in the arts. (Source: Radbourne, 1999).

such as a music performance, ballet, painting, ceramic pot, film, or designer clothing, its attributes to the marketplace lie in the intangible benefits to the individual customer.

Arts organizations learned the value of courting customers, knowing their customers and then satisfying their needs. This 'relationship' marketing transformed the arts marketing function of arts organizations and led to a new wave of arts marketing literature (Kotler & Scheff 1997, Kolb 2001, Colbert 2002, Hill and O'Sullivan 1995, Radbourne 1996, 1998 and 1999, Rentschler et al 2002). The shift from the transactional marketing of ticket selling and purchase, to relationship marketing and to loyalty marketing became more apparent as arts organizations learned more about engaging with their customers.

Figure 10.1 shows the strategies from Transactional marketing, through Relationship marketing to Loyalty marketing, that deepen audience or customer engagement with the product or company. Prospects become customers, subscribers and members as their relationship with the arts organization increases and the organization introduces new marketing objectives to meet new understandings of their customers or audience.

While this represents a shift from product orientation to customer orientation, it does not recognize the independence of individual consumers and their desire for greater personal involvement in an artistic experience. Loyalty is complex in the contemporary arts marketing environment. Customers have extraordinary choice. Their needs and values are individual, and the benefits of loyalty may not be worth the cost. The non-profit arts sector has been strengthened by loyal donors and advocates, however, new influences on consumers and new creative industries have changed the definition of relationship marketing towards a convergence of production and consumption.

The new consumer

Marketing in the arts is now driven by an audience quest for appropriation, connectivity and transformation through the arts experience. New immersive models of performance, presentation, production and distribution, are required in order to attract and retain audiences. Audiences want to be loyal and will be fiercely loyal if they can experience fulfilment and realization in the arts experience. Otherwise they are fickle – waiting for last minute options, time poor, with minimal expectations of satisfaction, and driven by peer pressure and short term relationships. This does not necessarily serve an arts organization's goal or mission. The performing arts risk sustainability without new relationships with the new consumer.

Art consumption is inherently experiential and the relationship between consumer and product has a cumulative effect on future consumption (Chong 2003).

The more you know, the more you appreciate it. This is to say that a self-reinforcing system exists: arts consumption increases with the ability to appreciate art, which is a function of past arts consumption. Satisfaction from arts consumption rises over time.

According to Chong, the art consumer has a relational bond to both the current product(s) and to the future production and consumption of like products. This is rationalized through personal taste and is realized through the stakeholder advantage such as advocacy and philanthropic donations.

This is further emphasized in the work of Lewis and Bridger (2001) who described the process of consumer need for self-actualization and quest for authenticity. They used four elements of the new consumers to build a new model of authentic loyalty based on authenticity. Consumers were described as individualistic, involved, independent and informed. They defined authenticity as a product or service that can be trusted to do what is claimed for it (p. 194). Importantly they described the personalization of authenticity arising out of each individual's personal experience and response. 'One cannot mass produce authenticity. Rather, it has to be introduced on an almost person-to-person basis, with individual needs, desires, expectations and interests being fully accounted for' (p.194). Audiences are consumers, and arts audiences clearly represent Lewis and Bridger's 'new consumer'. They have moved up Maslow's pyramid of human needs, seeking personal fulfilment in artistic experiences. They are intent on closing the gap between the person they are (the real self), and the person they want to be (the ideal self). This self-actualization is the outcome of the quest for authenticity. Lewis and Bridger claim that if the producer can meet the needs of consumers with authentic experiences (products and services), then authentic loyalty is achieved, which transcends the pseudo loyalty given by other consumers, easily tempted by better offers. The shift in the analysis of authenticity reflects a shift in focus from the authenticity of objects to the authenticity of subjects, and to the links between these two fields of relationship marketing and authenticity.

Other researchers in the consumer quest for authenticity (Cohen 1988 and Wang 1999) claim that authenticity is a quality perceived by individuals that emerges from their own personal experiences. They describe existential authenticity which is both intrapersonal and interpersonal. The first centres on the individual self and self-discovery and self-realization, and the second focuses on a collective sense of self where the experience brings individuals together to create witnesses to the self-experience, as in the collective audience attendance at a performance. The consumers' desire for authenticity stems from a drive for self-actualization, self-creation and self-realization: 'Hence, in the context of existential authenticity, individuals feel they are in touch both with a "real" world and with their "real" selves' (Leigh et al 2006: 483).

These claims are potent in the arts, where self-realization is the spiritual experience at the core of the arts product. The following model adapted from Lewis and Bridger (2001: 193) forms the basis for this analysis.

The two research studies that follow further support the concept of self-actualization as integral to relationship marketing in the performing arts. The author of this chapter was a chief investigator on both these Australian Research Council funded projects.

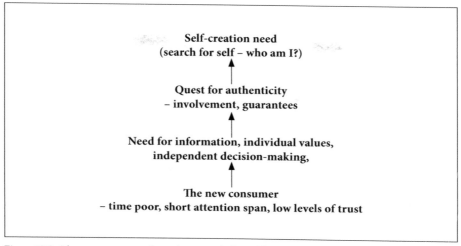

Figure 10.2: The consumer quest for authenticity. (Adapted from Lewis and Bridger, 2001).

Study 1: Talking Theatre

From 2004 to 2006 a longitudinal study *Talking Theatre*, conducted with fourteen performing arts centres in Queensland and the Northern Territory of Australia, was designed to build new audiences from deliberate engagement of non-theatregoers. The study replicated previous studies with the state opera company and two theatre companies, which had resulted in audience development strategies and new audiences. The key drivers of the study were sustainability of the regional performing arts centres and the development of a stronger relationship with the community. There was evidence of declining theatre audiences across regional Australia, minimal audience research at regional arts centres, limited marketing resources and increased competition for leisure spending. The research partners included the performing arts centres and the state/territory government agencies whose rationale for participation were the potential loyalty of audiences in communities and a government prioritization of regional development.

Non-theatregoers were invited to attend and experience three live performances at their local performing arts centre free of charge. In return, the participants agreed to complete a series of questionnaires and take part in post-performance discussions to share their reactions to the performances, to the venue and to theatregoing. Recruitment via local media resulted in a selection of 237 participants. Before their attendance, participants were asked to complete a questionnaire at home which included a combination of open and closed questions to derive demographic and psychographic information. Seventy-seven per cent of the sample respondents were male. Thirty-two per cent were aged 30 to 39 years, 23 per cent were aged 40 to 49 years and all were aged over 19 years and under 55 years. Fifty-six per cent had undertaken further study post secondary school. The most common occupation was parent or carer followed by employment in health, education, sales and administration. The average annual income was under AUD$50,000 p.a. Their preferred theatre entertainment was comedy, followed by popular and rock music. They commonly cited the ticket price as the reason for non-attendance.

These participants had never attended the local performing arts centre and their strongest expressed reason for attending was to 'have a good night out' (80 per cent) followed by 'to attend a quality show' (62 per cent). Participants could select more than one of six reasons (Scollen 2006: 53). Each of the performing arts centres selected a variety of genres of arts performances and experiences for participants such as plays, opera, contemporary dance, stand-up comedy, musicals, ballet and orchestra. Most of this was touring product, but included some locally produced performances.

Directly after experiencing each of the three performances, the participants individually completed the *Tonight's Performance* questionnaire in which they rated their experiences of the performance. The questionnaire consisted mostly of broad, closed questions to enable the same questionnaire to be completed by all participants regardless of the genres of performance attended. Of the aspects that helped participants enjoy the show, the most common response was the performers, and similarly, performers were rated as the most common aspect helping understanding of the show.

Participants then talked together in groups of twelve about their reception of the performance. The one-hour post-performance group discussions were audio-recorded and facilitated. The unstructured, free-flowing discussions generated substantial qualitative data that provided insight into the elements of performance and of theatregoing that were important to new audiences. A few weeks following the final *Talking Theatre* performance in each region another questionnaire was sent home for participants to complete. This *Feedback* questionnaire sought the participants' attitudes to the research, to their local performing arts centre, and to the possibility of future attendance. Fifty-seven per cent of the total sample sent back their completed questionnaires.

According to participant responses in the early post-performance discussions, one of the reasons many of the non-theatregoers avoided the performing arts centres was because they thought they would not enjoy or understand the performances. They assumed they would not be able to relate to anything in the performances, nor be able to relate to the other theatre patrons. This concern stemmed from their belief that theatre was elitist and catered for a certain type of person whose interests were different from theirs. They did not believe the experience would be 'authentic' or fit within their own measure of quality. However, enjoyment and comprehension levels were high and 54 per cent of the entire sample stated that they could relate to someone or something in the performances. In most cases this was the characters and the relationships between the characters in the performances. This indicated to these new audiences that the cultures represented on stage were not different from their own cultures. Comments about the similarity of the paying audience members to themselves were also consistently made in the post-performance group discussions.

Participants noted the 'smart-casual' attire of the theatre patrons as opposed to the formality that they had expected. They noted the variety of age ranges present and saw many audience members who appeared to be a similar age to themselves. The participants were also pleasantly surprised to see children and families at the theatre because many had assumed that children would not be welcome in this perceived formal adult environment. Through this self-discovery, a new self-creation was emerging.

These discoveries assisted the non-theatregoers to feel more confident about the prospect of future theatre attendance because many of their initial concerns were diminished. It also illustrated that the performing arts centres were presenting appropriate live performances for this target market, with which they were readily able to engage. The findings pointed to the elements in performance that were most engaging for new audiences, as well as indicating the areas of concern that had prevented their attendance in the past.

Price played a significant part in determining theatre attendance, however, all participants stated they would be willing to spend more than $45 per ticket on a performance if they really wanted to see it (mostly concerts, opera, ballet, musicals or comedians). They would pay top ticket price if they had positive expectations of the experience, an understanding of what the show would be like, had heard plenty of word-of-mouth recommendations or knew about it from television, were convinced that it would entertain, and so believed that it would be worth spending the money. In many cases, the participants could appreciate the value in the ticket prices after directly experiencing the performances in the project. The experience of the live performances and of the 'highly-skilled' and 'charismatic' performers convinced most of the non-theatregoers that the ticket prices were appropriate. It was also quite common for the non-theatregoers to presume ticket prices were expensive. However, they were pleasantly surprised to discover that some of the performances at the performing arts centres were less expensive than they had thought.

Relationship marketing is at the heart of the *Talking Theatre* strategy. Through consultation, relationship building, knowledge transfer, and trust, new audiences were developed. However a deeper analysis of the participants' needs or expectations reveals that they are close to Wang's definition of existential authenticity, which centres on self-discovery and self-realization in the presence of others. The study showed that many non-theatregoers in regional areas are potential new audiences. They are interested in attending live performances and when introduced to the activity they enjoy the experience. However, non-theatregoers are often unsure of what to expect from theatregoing and do not have respected peers to encourage them to attend. *Talking Theatre* provided the opportunity to introduce people to their local performing arts centre, to make them feel valued and welcome, and to assist them to learn about theatregoing through direct experience, self-reflection and peer review.

There were also economic outcomes. The *Talking Theatre* project generated a 110 per cent increase in ticket purchases by all participants. Twenty-nine per cent of all participants returned more than once to their regional performing arts centre. In addition, the performing arts centres were given the opportunity to showcase their organizations and product to potential new audiences, to learn from their unique perspectives, and to foster ongoing relationships with them and their social networks. The local and state government departments were given feedback of the needs of the regional performing arts sector and of non-theatregoers living in regional areas. This informed policies and investments to create greater participation in the arts.

Study 2: Deep Blue orchestra

A second study involved developing a new orchestral model to explore new product development in music which linked the development of new repertoire in response to expressed audience needs and desires. The experiment in Brisbane, Australia, involved building a test orchestra called Deep Blue, and presenting an eclectic selection of existing works and new compositions with projected visual images, player involvement and audience involvement, no conductor, no music stands, and a shared performance and audience space.

Primary research through focus groups with the audience and the Deep Blue musicians, and through an audience survey, showed that the audience enjoyed the interaction between the performers and themselves, positively describing the experience of no barriers, the live enthusiasm, the feeling of engagement and stretching the boundaries of their relationship with music. Audiences said that the performance mirrored the changes and challenges of life in the early 21st century. They talked about the animation of the musicians generating energy, and the appeal of the physical staging, and wanted a more innovative repertoire to match this. The survey revealed that music is a personal experience provoking an emotional response, yet participated in with friends. This audience claimed that they would not buy a CD of the performance, but that the venue, ambience, and audience behaviour were contributors to a particular experience.

The Deep Blue musicians enjoyed the freedom, innovation, diversity, and audience interactivity of this orchestral performance model. They wanted to be able to share intellectually, emotionally and physically with the audience, as the response factor was needed for their best performance. They revealed a need for greater interaction with the other performers in order to heighten interaction with the audience. The musicians also wanted some ownership of, and involvement in, the production process. This posed new thinking for intellectual property and content development. These findings demonstrated that audiences and musicians wanted a kind of connectivity in production and performance.

Further audience research using the same survey questions and focus group questions was conducted with two other classical (Maestro concert) and popular (Sci-Fi concert) orchestral performances by the established Queensland Orchestra, the state symphony orchestra. Respondents totalled 298. In all concerts, the musicians/performers were considered the best element of the performance. Irrespective of the different audience demographics, it was important for people to connect and engage with the performing artists. The question about buying a CD/DVD of the performance showed that for all the concerts, this was not a very high priority for the audience, highlighting the importance of attending a live performance which provides more of an 'experience'. Overall, most audiences responded that they would come again to such a performance.

Respondents were asked to describe the role of the audience in a musical performance from a list of six roles: spectator, emotional listener, passive listener, co-producer, active participant, or other. The highest response for every concert, that is, type of orchestral performance surveyed, was 'emotional listener'. Question 10 in the survey presented a series of statements with which respondents rated their agreement, from strongly disagree to strongly agree, as follows.

Table 10.1: Question 10 in Deep Blue/Queensland Orchestra audience survey

Integration of visual images and sound facilitates a greater enjoyment of music.	1	2	3	4	5
A person's musical background and experience influences their expectations of a musical performance.	1	2	3	4	5
A musical performance evokes an emotional response in the audience.	1	2	3	4	5
Pre-performance information is important to enjoyment of a musical performance.	1	2	3	4	5
The context (venue, ambience, behaviour of audience) contributes to the experience of a music performance.	1	2	3	4	5
Interaction between the audience and performers results in audience enjoyment.	1	2	3	4	5

The third statement, seeking a rating about emotional response to a musical performance, received significantly higher agreement than all the others. Table 10.2 summarizes key respondent answers to the experiential audience role.

Table 10.2: Orchestral audience responses on experiential authenticity

Question	Maestro concert n = 30	Deep Blue concert n = 220	Sci-Fi concert n = 48
Role of the audience in a musical performance nominated as 'emotional listener'.	73.8%	64%	77%
A musical performance evokes an emotional response in the audience (mean score on scale 1–5).	4.49	4.05	4.41

Although the concert repertoire, venues and productions were quite different, it appears that an emotional connection was established with the audience, irrespective of the style of music and performance. Self-actualization, or a discovery of self, was therefore common for all music attendees. Cross tabulation with musical preference, repertoire, age, education, or occupation showed no significant difference in responses.

The influence of the social network in the orchestral experience was demonstrated by the way people find out about a concert and also in the way they attend a concert. The findings suggested that the information needs of the performing arts consumer can be captured in the shared experience. Attending the concert with friends was the most popular way for all three concert audiences and this information can be used to build relationship marketing strategies.

These two studies revealed that the performing arts audience is discerning and prepared to take risks if they can be involved. They want to participate and be free to express their engagement. They value innovation and the new technologies, and are interested in new repertoire and new musical and sensory experiences. They want input in the production process. This directly represents Lewis and Bridger's description of the consumer quest for authenticity: the desire to be involved in the process of production and consumption, wanting an individual experience, making the decision to engage independently, and seeking information when making the decision to attend. The search for authenticity is a search for an original, unique and personal experience, that fulfils a spiritual quest for actualization which is the 'emotional response' role attributed to and by the audiences in these studies.

The creative process

Relationship marketing strategies cannot completely fulfil this quest, because the strategies are based on what the organization or the product can do for the consumer. They do not fulfil the basic need for self-creation through the arts experience. It is important to note, however, that there is a strong link between the creative process of the artist, and the self actualization of the need for self-creation by the consumer.

The following figure is based on Throsby's description (2001: 96) of the creative process in his discourse of cultural value. He describes a pure creativity model where the artist conceives the idea and executes the work for no other purpose than the value of that art to the self, the artist. When external influences are involved, the artist is influenced by other values. Technical constraints, time in labour, and the number of works are the variables that may influence the process. When economic values are added to the creative process, such as income generation and costs of producing the work, the creative process is confronted by the demands of the market for the work. Throsby interprets the artistic work as supplying a dual market, where consumers give the work an economic value and an aesthetic value.

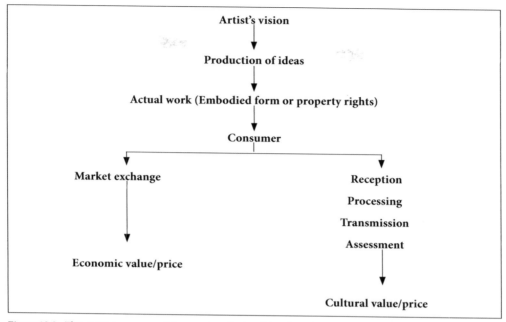

Figure 10.3: The creative process and the creation of value. (Based on Throsby's description of the creative process, 2001).

In this figure, the consumer plays a role in defining the value of the artistic creation, yet, for the consumer, the arts experience is image-based and arises from self-determination. The utilitarian or investment quality of an artistic creation redefines the product and its value. For the artist, the 'market' is the key in attributing value to the work. The dilemma is how the consumer, as co-creator, makes this decision.

Florida (2002: 165–189) presented a different but compelling argument for consumers searching for a creative experience. His conclusion that the creative class crave a life 'packed full of intense, high-quality, multidimensional experiences' and consume experience in this way, is not defined by the value placed on creative work nor by a collaboration or convergence with the artist or creative worker's moment of creative idea generation or production.

Convergence is defined by Hesmondhalgh (2002) in various ways, to demonstrate how the term has been used in the cultural industries. Convergence of cultural forms has been used to describe the multimedia convergence of music, sounds, words, images and texts. Convergence of corporate ownership defines the breaking down of boundaries between media, telecommunications and computing. Convergence of communication systems is used to describe networked personal computers with other media technologies (p. 221). This chapter adds a new use of 'convergence': convergence of creator and consumer. This is the basis for the new marketing model which takes Florida's positioning of the creative class as craving a creative experience in their consumption activity, to the basis of a new marketing paradigm in arts marketing.

The figure essentially overlays the creative process with the self-actualization process of the new consumer and shows there is a convergence of interdependence at every stage of creative product development and every stage of consumer engagement. The new consumer (or arts audience member) demands a customized experience which is personal but in the company of others, meets quality expectations and can be consumed where the audience is located. As engagement grows, expectations are met and interdependence increases. The consumer/audience demands collaboration or partnership where invitations are personalized and information shared and used in decision-making about the level of engagement. At the highest level of engagement the consumer/audience demands to be heard, providing feedback directly to the artist or creator or via a committee or blog on the authenticity and intrinsic benefits of the experience, exposing self-actualization needs and possibly influencing artistic programming or the creative conceptualization. Creativity and marketing converge in this new engagement with audiences.

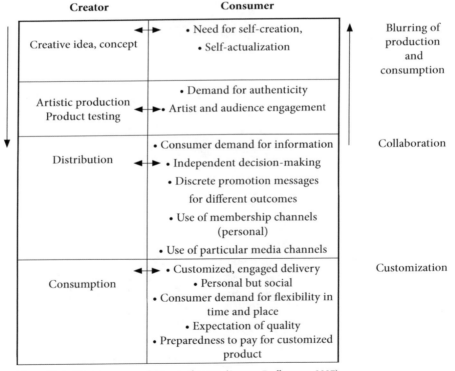

Figure 10.4: Convergence marketing in the arts. (Source: Radbourne, 2007).

Conclusion

This chapter has attempted to show that the new consumer in the arts requires a new marketing paradigm. In this paradigm, the creative process and the consumer's quest for self-actualization through the artistic or cultural experience converge. The creative process is completed by a shared journey to market and aesthetic value which engages the individual consumer in the artistic idea, the prototype testing, the production, and the consumption. The term 'consumer' may more comfortably be 'participant' or 'partner'. Relationship marketing strategies suffice if they are not organization-focused, but a more obvious sharing of an authentic experience. Inherently, this marketing relationship has no boundaries; it is built on networks, interaction and collaboration. Ultimately, the creative process is strengthened by this engagement.

I wish to acknowledge Professor Andy Arthurs, Shari Lindblom and Dr Rebecca Scollen for their work in the research studies described in this chapter.

References

Chong, D. (2005), 'Stakeholder Relationships in the Market for Contemporary Art', in I. Robertson (ed.), *Understanding International Art Markets and Management*, London: Routledge, pp. 84–102.

Cohen, E. (1988), 'Authenticity and the Commoditization of Tourism', *Annals of Tourism Research*, 15, pp. 371–386.

Colbert, F. (2006), *Marketing Culture and the Arts*, Montreal: HEC.

Florida, R. (2002), *The Rise of the Creative Class*, New York: Basic Books.

Hesmondhalgh, D. (2002), *The Cultural Industries*, London: Sage.

Hill, E., O'Sullivan, C. & O'Sullivan, T. (1995), *Creative Arts Marketing*, Oxford: Butterworth Heinemann.

Kolb, B. (2001), 'The Decline of the Subscriber Base: A Study of the Philharmonia Orchestra Audience', *International Journal of Arts Management*, 3: 2, pp. 51–59.

Kotler, P. & Scheff, J. (1997), *Standing Room Only: Strategies for Marketing the Performing Arts*, Boston: Harvard Business School Press.

Leigh, T. W., Peters, C. & Shelton, J. (2006), 'The Consumer Quest for Authenticity: The Multiplicity of Meanings within the MG Subculture of Consumption', *Journal of the Academy of Marketing Science*, 34: 4, pp. 481–493.

Lewis, D. & Bridger, D. (2001), *The Soul of the New Consumer*, London: Nicholas Brealey Publishing.

Newman, D. (1996), *Subscribe Now*, New York: Theatre Communications Group Inc. (Eighth printing).

Radbourne, J. (1998), 'The Role of Government in Marketing the Arts', *The Journal of Arts Management, Law and Society*, 28: 1 (Spring), pp. 67–82.

Radbourne, J. & Fraser, M. (1996), *Arts Management – A Practical Guide,* Sydney: Allen & Unwin.

Rentschler, R., Radbourne, J., Carr, R. & Rickard, J. (2002), 'Relationship Marketing and Performing Arts Organization Viability', *International Journal of Nonprofit & Public Sector Marketing,* 7: 2, pp. 118–130.

Scheff Bernstein, J. (2007), *Arts Marketing Insights,* San Francisco: John Wiley and Sons Inc.

Scollen, R. (2006), *New Audiences, New Relationships ... Three Years in Review,* Final Report to Australian Research Council, Northern Australia Regional Performing Arts Centres Association, Arts Queensland, Arts Northern Territory and Queensland University of Technology, Brisbane: Queensland University of Technology.

Throsby, D. (2001), *Economics and Culture,* Cambridge: Cambridge University Press.

Wang, N. (1999), 'Rethinking Authenticity in Tourism Experience', *Annals of Tourism Research,* 26: 2, pp. 349–370.

Chapter 11

Listening to the Audience: Methods for a New Era of Audience
Research

Katya Johanson

C Almost all theories of art that have ever been proposed make some kind of reference to an audience', Zangwill wrote in 1999. Knowledge of the audience would thus seem to be central not only to the practice of the performing arts, but also to arts scholarship (Zangwill 1999: 315). Indeed, arts organizations and funding agencies have for many years collected survey data on the constitution and behaviour of audiences. In the past decade, arts marketers (e.g., Baxter 2010; Brown & Novak 2007), policy-makers (Keaney 2008) and practitioners have advocated for, commissioned or conducted studies that examine the motivations of audience members in attending a performance, and their experience of an arts event both during and after it. The interest in audience research that unites the chapters in this book is part of a growing international scholarly interest in the *experience of audiences* as opposed to a study of who audiences are, in terms of the class, ethnic background or social group they represent.

Yet until recently much of the impetus for audience research in the performing arts has come from the theatre companies or funding agencies, rather than from academic scholarship (Bennett 2006; Sauter 2002). Instead, theatre scholars have preferred to critically analyse the text of the performance. Bennett suggests that the emphasis paid to text in performing arts research is inconsistent with the nature of the art form, because the production itself relies on interaction with the audience, and therefore has an inherently social nature. Rather than aligning themselves with text-based research and imagining an ideal audience, Bennett suggests, performing arts researchers should find correlation in social science research, in order to go out and investigate audiences (Bennett 1997: 212). Freshwater, too, notes that qualitative research into theatre audiences is lacking: 'Whereas researchers working on television and film engage with audiences through surveys, in-depth interviews, and ethnographic research, almost no one in theatre studies seems to be interested in exploring what actual audiences members make of a performance' (Freshwater 2009: 29). Instead, 'theatre scholars seem to be more comfortable making strong assertions about theatre's unique influence and impact on the audiences than gathering and assessing the evidence which might support these claims' (Freshwater 2009: 3–4).

These authors argue that the absence of scholarly audience research reflects assumptions that researchers make about audiences. Freshwater, for example, argues that such reluctance to investigate audiences is not simply a widespread oversight, but reflects a 'suspicion of the mass audience' that is 'sustained by twenty-first century fears about the ignorance and malevolence that may be contained within the anonymous populace, and it also has roots which lie buried deep among much longer-lived cultural anxieties' (Freshwater 2008: 38; on music, see also Pitts 2005). Where audience research has been conducted, it has been criticized for its lack of attention to issues of methodology, and its lack of rigour. Bennett (1997) and Butsch (2008) argue that historically, the people who have collected information about audiences tend to be well-educated, with a substantial bank of cultural capital. Their representation of the appropriate terms and conditions for audience engagement has tended to reflect their class interests rather than the experience of the audience members themselves (Butsch 2008: 3–4). Scollen notes that theatre audience research tends to focus on regular theatregoers rather than non-theatregoers (2007), again perhaps reflecting the preconceptions of researchers rather than the reality of attendance characteristics. In the parallel field of cultural studies, Barker argues that audience studies fail to investigate or employ 'checkable' methodologies, and such research commonly represents an accumulation of detail: 'We "tell interesting stories" of particular texts and audiences and contexts. Nothing wrong with these, but they just don't amount to more than onion soup' (Barker 2006: 129).

Such allegations that too little attention has been paid to the audience and that what attention has been paid has been influenced by the unchecked biases of researchers suggest that more comprehensive attention to appropriate data collection methods is at least one of the requirements for improving the rigour, quality and extent of research on audience engagement. To shift from a focus on arts production or audience demographics to the audience experience requires research that looks beyond the presence of the audience member in the theatre or concert hall (Bennett 1997; Foreman-Wernet 2009), to examine the audience member's experience, cultural influences on that experience and its ongoing nature after the participant has left the theatre (Barker 2006). This need to understand audiences – rather than take them for granted as the passive recipients of an artist's expertly prepared offering – is all the greater in an era in which audiences are engaging actively in critiquing, creating and co-creating performances.

This chapter serves as a conclusion to the book by providing a survey of research methods that have been employed in this collection and elsewhere, to identify, describe and evaluate the audience experience. It is not concerned with advocating for one methodological framework over another, agreeing with Press that 'our methodological rifts', such as those between advocates of quantitative or qualitative research, 'have outlived their usefulness' (Press 2006: 98). Rather, the chapter reviews the use of a range of methods by arts audience researchers to identify the strengths and weaknesses of each, including conventional and more innovative methods and the shift to a methodological approach that attempts to incorporate the knowledge gained from qualitative research to more comprehensive quantitative surveys.

Methods of qualitative research from the social sciences

Qualitative studies of audiences include the conventional techniques of social science research, such as collecting information from interviews and focus groups. These studies are often framed by discourse analysis and borrow heavily from reception theory. Such methods are regarded as giving the researcher the capacity to 'elucidate the subjective and elusive' concepts associated with the audience's experience (Walmsley 2011: 6). Willmar Sauter's 'Theatre Talks' techniques, for example, were developed in the 1980s and provided a variation on the focus group model, which followed the following principles: (1) group discussions were held immediately following a performance so that the participants' views could not be affected by influences they encountered after leaving the theatre; (2) participants were selected on the basis that they all either know each other or were homogeneous in terms of education and/or employment sector, on the grounds that theatre attendance is a social experience and people with much in common were more likely to chat after a performance; and (3) the group moderator would maintain minimal engagement in the conversation, so as not to lead the conversation (Sauter 2002; Scollen 2007).

Focus groups and interviews rely inherently on the assumption that what people say is what they mean. While this might seem to be a reasonable assumption, there are several reasons to doubt the accuracy of the research participants' verbal reports. Baxter identifies some of these: '[T]here is a danger that the responses could be influenced by partial memory (e.g., not being able to recall significant habitual or spontaneous events or behaviours), cognitive filters such as selective memory (sharing only what they think the researcher believes important) and peer pressure (succumbing to social mores, wanting to project an idealized self and the desire to simply "give a good answer")' (Baxter 2010: 131; see also Schoenmakers and Tulloch 2004: 15). In his chapter in this book, Matthew Reason identifies a potential case in which focus group participants all appeared to form their answers in order to rebel against rather than please the researcher.

Discourse analysis suggests also that the act of talking about the feelings associated with an audience experience brings those experiences into being, so it is when given the opportunity to speak that the audience actually has the experience, albeit retrospectively. If the benefit of research is measured by its capacity to directly contribute to the depth of the audience's experience, this consequence of soliciting a narrative account is no bad outcome. Throughout audience research conducted by Radbourne et al. (2009), audience participants in focus groups often expressed gratitude to the focus group conductor for the opportunity to reflect on the performance and to share their experience in a group, and this benefit of research participation is also supported by Reason's reflections on his experience (2010 and in this volume). In a sense, participants experience the focus group as an extension of the artistic event itself because this experience is inherently social, and so post-performance research can heighten their experience of that event.

However, for the purpose of research itself, the use of conventional qualitative 'talk-based' techniques risks both limiting the results to that which can be articulated and increasing the significance of the experience by providing such a forum for expression and social interaction. In Radbourne et al.'s (2009, 2010) research, it was common to find that focus-group participants became more expressive and loquacious as the focus group proceeded, which was no doubt partly as their social confidence with one another improved, but may also have been due to the fact that the experience of the performance they had seen was becoming more significant to them in the course of discussion. The research participant's experience is constrained by their vocabulary, and without a 'specialist vocabulary the very attempt to reflect can override our ability to know our own mind' (Reason 2010: 17).

This relationship between cause and effect is an issue facing all social science researchers, but is arguably more problematic in audience research than in other forms of qualitative research, due to the limitations of our vocabulary in describing the often ineffable and intangible qualities of our experience. This represents a substantial methodological problem for the researcher: 'If the experience of a performance is what was taking place back there and then, in the auditorium, then the researcher's very attempt to access this through (self-) conscious reflections on the experience after the event might itself disrupt participants' ability to know their own feelings' (Reason 2010: 18). The capacity to 'lead' research participants jeopardizes the validity of the research.

Complicating this relationship between the experience of, and reporting on, audience experience is the fact that, as Antoine Hennion (2001) and Stephanie Pitts (2005) have noted, 'people are now so "sociologized"' (Hennion 2201: 5) and knowledgeable about research techniques that respondents are 'engaged in a certain degree of self-presentation, conveying their own interpretations of their attitudes and experiences as part of their response' (Pitts 2005: 259). The meta-cognitive approach that participants might take to the research means that they are more likely to either give the researcher what they think he or she wants or expects, or to deliberately withhold such information.

Researchers have developed strategies to avoid this behaviour, such as 'adept reframing of the research question that throws a "curve ball" at participants, encouraging them to avoid the obvious or stereotypical answer; or facilitation techniques that develop a conducive, positive group dynamic where mutual trust and respect are engendered' (Baxter 2010: 132). Sauter's 'Theatre Talks' avoids the propensity of research participants to check their answers before speaking by having the moderator not ask questions, but rather encourage participants to talk freely (Sauter 2002: 124). Yet the limitation of such a strategy is that it is designed only for research in which a broad range of topics is appropriate, because the moderator cannot direct the conversation.

Another method of data collection is the use of online blogs or other forms of social media to invite written audience responses to a performance. In terms of the kind of data to which this method gives rise, the outcome is very similar to focus groups, except that it also has the benefit of attracting long-term cumulative contributions rather than a one-off event. As a result, it can potentially respond to Barker's (2006) point that the experience of the audience member continues long after the evening of the performance. It also has the benefit of providing anonymity to the blog contributor, which in the case of some participants may lead to a more accurate report on their experience as they feel less inhibited by the social interaction of the group or the expectations of the researcher. Radbourne et al. (2010) identify the use of online blogs as a form of 'deep research' because each response has the capacity to build on those before it, providing multiple layers of information. However, Fearon cautions that there is bias in the collection of data from blogs, as they represent not a random sample of audience members, but rather they attract the conventional supporters of the theatre company: '[T]he blogs of theatre companies are frequently anodyne and do not seem to be accessed outside industry or educational elites ... the demographic representation of bloggers is never clear, and therefore cannot be argued to be completely representative. Reviews, blogs, letters or journals are disproportionally representative of industry or educational elites, and therefore undervalue or even ignore the real audience experience' (Fearon 2010: 132). If this is indeed the case, the use of such new technologies may simply reinforce the existing habits that Bennett and Butsch identify, in which researchers rich in cultural capital study audience members who are equally rich in cultural capital.

Innovative qualitative methods of audience research

The suggestion in the discussion above is that researchers cannot entirely rely on oral or written accounts of the audience's experience to provide a whole picture of this experience. If there is much about the audience experience that is affective rather than cognitive, then conventional 'talk-based' research is limited when 'trying to explore less tangible lines of investigation such as brand resonance, the intangibles of an arts experience, the hidden drivers behind decision making or the subtle dimensions of a person's relationship with the arts' (Baxter 2010: 312). Researchers have responded to this perceived inadequacy by using techniques that are non-verbal and/or more immediate than post-show participant reports. Research may be conducted during the performance through the use of customized technologies to gauge audience members' levels of emotion or engagement (such as by pushing buttons at times of heightened engagement, or by monitoring the participant's heart rate or neurological activity), or through the less-technological methods of participant observation or ethnography.

The advantage of observational and ethnographic approaches is that they have the capacity to respond to the fact that the audience experience is not simply a visual or auditory processing of the performance, but can be a 'whole body' experience. Reason notes:

> The audience experience might also be considered an intersubjective doing, through kinaesthetic empathy with the movement and presence of people in space. Each of these possibilities constructs the audience experience as something embodied, something present in descriptions of audiences as not just watching and listening to a performance with their eyes and ears but *experiencing* it with their whole bodies.
>
> (Reason 2010: 20)

In recognition of this 'whole body reaction', Hagnell examined children's reactions to a performance by using a split television screen to simultaneously view both the children in the audience and the action on stage screen (see Sauter 2002: 120). Witnessing audience members' physical and physiognomic responses to a performance can provide an affective dimension to research. Such ethnographic study resembles the informal information-collection habits of experienced theatre employees, who are accustomed to 'reading' the temperament of an audience in the theatre foyer. Fearon argues also that ethnographic analysis succeeds in representing the audience where other research methods – in which we might include interviews and focus groups – have failed because they have privileged the views and expressions of audience members who are capable of recognizing, accepting and articulating the theatre company's 'preferred reading'. Interviews and focus-group methods produce an incomplete picture of the audience's experience, and one that errs on the side of those who feel themselves to be 'in the know': an articulate and positive reception. 'Without detailed ethnographic analysis of audiences we are inevitably reliant on the reading of critics, whereas the reception of the "real" audience must contain a variety of readings, including the negotiated, oppositional or incompetent' (Fearon 2010: 133).

Techniques such as these are likely to become more popular and more important to audience research as audiences increasingly become creators. Performances that incorporate willing audience members are becoming more common. At the 2012 Adelaide Fringe Festival (Australia), for example, the More than Opera company ran a show called 'Sing Your Own Wagner Chorus with the Three Maestri', in which participants were called for from the general public and, after a series of workshops, were invited to perform in a public concert. The alacrity with which such opportunities are adopted and the possibilities that they offer for observation will provide fertile material for future scholarship, just as audiences become performers and researchers become the audience.

The methodological criticisms that tend to be levelled at observational research lie in the ethical implications – an issue Sauter raised with Hagnell's use of television to view children as audiences – and in the fact that such research has in the past tended to exaggerate the power and inclination of the 'active audience' who can engage or not engage with a performance at will (Morley 2006; Barker 2006). This latter criticism is partly directed at the researcher's preconceptions, and recent ethnographic research on audiences has made efforts to avoid such assumptions. In her application of Hall's 'encoding/decoding' media studies approach to live performing arts audience research, for instance, Fearon introduces the notion of the 'incompetent' reader (audience member) as an addition to Hall's typology of reader responses. The 'incompetent' reader is one who, as a result of their educational or cultural background, is not able to engage with the performance. With this addition, Fearon avoids the charge that ethnographic research romanticizes the supposed power of the audience and imagines that it can 'constantly produce oppositional readings' (Morley 2006: 102–103) and draws research attention to subjects of interest to theatre companies: the reluctant audience member.

Yet such a charge also points to the difficulty associated with ethnographic study, in that active physiognomic or physiological responses to a performance are more visible and arguably easier to interpret than less active responses, and therefore provide more compelling data for the researcher. A practical limitation of ethnographic audience research is that it is not possible to generalize from specific ethnographic research to speak about audiences as a larger group. Morley cautions: 'Ethnography is a fine thing, but it always runs the danger of descending into anecdotalism and we should not mistake the vividness of the examples it offers us for their general applicability. Indeed the process of extrapolation from ethnographic examples is one that always needs to be handled with particular care' (Morley 2006: 106). The accusation that ethnography easily romanticises the power of the audience indicates the substantial role that interpretation plays in the research.

A method that shares with ethnography the capacity to track affective response is the collection of continual audience responses, delivered by technologies throughout a performance, such as a computer device that allows audiences to register feelings of excitement. These technologies have been readily adopted by art forms in which the audience's response is likely to vary throughout the performance, such as dance or music. Vincs et al. asked audience members to use a 'portable audience response facility' to probe and map 'the ways in which our conceptual understanding of, and hence responses to, dance are structured as dance unfolds' on a moment-by-moment basis (2010: 360). This technique provides a simple form of quantitative data, valuable for analysis when responses provide a pattern; Vincs et al. were able to identify 'gem moments' (2010: 358), although they noted that the participants in their study – dance students and artists – all shared a reasonably high level of acquaintance with dance (Vincs et al. 2009: 5). As with many quantitative techniques, the use of the portable device allowed the researchers to identify when the audience was engaged with the dance, but not necessarily what factors contributed to that engagement, and the authors were cautious not to extrapolate too much about the choreography that coincided with 'gem moments'.

A potentially more expressive strategy is the post-performance technique of eliciting creative responses from audience members, such as drawings or movement, which represent participants' affective reactions to an artistic event. In Baxter's (2010: 132) terms, these are '[s]marter methods … to take the research inquiry beyond "harvesting" conscious information to "mining" for beyond conscious insights'. Respondents need not rely on the limited capacity of language necessary for a 'standard question and answer format', but rather, such research might give the researcher 'an understanding about what role the arts or a specific cultural offer plays in the creation and expression of a person's multiple social and personal identities; or attain a sophisticated perspective on people's attitudes, perceptions and needs in relation to the arts and begin to appreciate the degree to which the arts resonate with their beliefs and values' (Baxter 2010: 133). These research techniques are useful in comparison to conventional 'talking strategies' when the participants' language skills are limited, as in the case of children. They also reflect the fact that audience members not only all have individual experiences, but also that each audience member might have a range of responses to a performance. It is common, for example, for an audience member to feel anticipation at the beginning of a performance, fear for the characters in the middle of a performance, get distracted before the interval and delight at the resolution and pleasure at the end. Such a range might be better represented in a picture or enactment than in a one-answer-per-question focus group.

Yet once again, it is likely that the researcher can infer a participant's response to a performance from a drawing more accurately when the participant shares cultural or social characteristics with the researcher, than when the two have little in common. Whether or not such research can be guaranteed to be any less biased than conventional qualitative research is arguable. Leaving aside specific audience demographic groups, such as children, if 'talk-based' research strategies attract and privilege the views of people with extensive cultural capital, then requesting participants to draw a picture to illustrate their experience of the performance is likely to have a similar effect.

Furthermore, the motives of researchers engaged in such studies often include a desire to promote the experience of an audience at a particular event. Ratsoy (2008), for example, reports on an exhibition she devised with James Hoffman of photographs of audience members of Kamloops's Western Canada Theatre, as part of an extensive audience research project. The purposes of this exhibition were 'manifold', but the first-listed purpose was to 'celebrate a company – and its loyal audience – that has been playing an instrumental role in the cultural life of a community for more than three decades' (Ratsoy 2008: 9). Whether or not a public exhibition of audience members is genuinely capable of adopting a critical approach to, say, the company's programme from the audience members' perspective was not broached. The aim of this audience research is in fact both to celebrate and perhaps heighten the experience of the 'loyal audience' and to serve as promotion: both worthy aims but not ones that complement a critical approach.

This chapter began by noting the now prevalent argument that the audience has been all too absent from past scholarly performing arts studies and that where it has received attention such research has been biased by the cultural interests of researchers. A recurring theme of the chapter has been the difficult act of interpretation in many of the qualitative methods discussed, including the conventional social science 'talk-based' techniques, the use of written accounts (blogs), ethnographic and observational techniques and the collection of creative responses to a performance.

Incorporating quantitative methods in audience research

In recent years there have been a few initiatives that attempt to take the knowledge gained about the audience experience from existing qualitative research to construct quantitative research tools. Quantitative data, such as box office reports and customer surveys, have long been collected to establish *who* goes to a performance, or sometimes only who pays, but now quantitative techniques such as surveys are increasingly used to identify not only the age profile, education level, income and home-suburb of the audience, but to establish patterns in the audience's experience of performance. Brown and Novak's 2007 study of the intrinsic impact of live performance used pre- and post-performance questionnaires with audiences at 19 performances ranging from popular Broadway theatre to orchestral concerts. The study examined both the participants' 'readiness to receive' an impact from the performance – thereby providing a nuanced set of distinctions between what Fearon (2010) would call 'negotiated, oppositional and incompetent' readers – and the intrinsic impact of the performance. The intrinsic impact included the extent to which the audience was captivated, intellectually stimulated, found emotional resonance, spiritual value, aesthetic growth and social bonding through their experience at the performance. As the questionnaire's architects, the researchers were able to guide responses in a way that was not possible with Sauter's Theatre Talks. Participants were able to respond anonymously and without the social inhibitions or motives that are prevalent in focus groups and creative response techniques.

A recent study by Radbourne et al. (2010) examined how four indicators of audience experience contributed to engagement, using a survey of audiences at performances by six small-to-medium Australian performing arts companies. By 2010, the survey had been collected from over 800 audience members and investigated the audience's sense of engagement, authenticity of the performance, the risk they experienced and their need for prior knowledge.

The use of quantitative surveys to gather such nuanced information also has methodological limitations. While Brown and Novak found that they were able to measure intrinsic impact and to establish that different performances created different sets of impact, they were only partially able to prove their third hypothesis: that high levels of readiness do not always result in higher impact. They noted that impact 'is simply too unpredictable, and too much depends on the performance itself' (Brown and Novak 2007: 19). Quantitative studies have lent themselves to measuring levels of impact or engagement, but have not necessarily been able to establish the factors that contribute to that engagement. As with the Brown and Novak study, the challenge for the Radbourne et al. study was to ask 'simple and intuitive questions about complex and abstract constructs' (Brown and Novak 2007: 21). If, as Hennion argues, research participants have become 'sociologized', it is also true that their expectations of a survey have been set by earlier surveys they have experienced, and participants in the Radbourne et al. research found the survey 'superficial' rather than straightforward. This is perhaps because they expected a more qualitative investigation of their response to the content of the performance or artistic qualities of a specific performance. Indeed, many respondents used the 'Other Comments' facility of the survey to contribute more in-depth but unsolicited qualitative feedback on the performance. It may be that more instruction about the purpose of the survey is required until the time comes, as Brown and Novak suggest it will, when 'a simple two-page questionnaire is administered routinely after performances' (2007: 21).

Conclusion

Performing arts scholarship has recently turned its attention towards research that examines not only who constitutes the audience but also what they experience in a performance, and how they feel about that experience. This turn marks an exciting time for audience research, because it recognizes that the actual audience is more complex and interesting than the ideal audience that has long received the attention of theatre scholars. Ironically, the interest in the audience as a subject of scholarly research coincides with the disintegration of clear boundaries between the audience and the performer, as audiences seek to become more actively involved in production. The complexity of the performing arts audience lies in the fact that their experience includes both cognitive and affective responses, varies through the course of a performance as well as from one audience member to the next, and begins before they enter the theatre and continues long after they leave. This complexity makes the appropriate research method for studying the audience an important issue.

On the one hand, conventional qualitative 'talk-based' techniques play to the criticism that they privilege the views of the experienced and articulate theatregoer rather than the traditional non-attender. Arts researchers have developed innovative alternatives to these conventional techniques, which are designed to capture affective responses, including monitoring 'whole body' reactions and inviting creative responses to a performance. Such techniques require extensive interpretation and are arguably no more successful in avoiding research bias than conventional techniques. A third camp of techniques involves using conventional quantitative techniques such as surveys, but to measure responses to performance rather than characteristics of the audience member. The challenge for the researcher of the audience experience is perhaps not to select the most appropriate technique, but to identify an appropriate combination of techniques.

References

Abercrombie, N. & Longhurst, B. (1998), *Audiences: A Sociological Theory of Performance and Imagination*, London: Sage.

Barker, M. (2003), 'Crash, Theatre Audiences, and the Idea of "Liveness"', *Studies in Theatre and Performance*, 23: 1, pp. 21–39.

Baxter, L. (2010), 'From Luxury to Necessity: The Changing Role of Qualitative Research in the Arts', in D. O'Reilly & F. Kerrigan (eds), *Marketing the Arts*, Abingdon Oxon: Routledge, pp. 121–140.

Bennett, S. (1997), *Theatre Audiences: A Theory of Production and Reception*, second edition, London and New York: Routledge.

——— (2000), 'Theatre Audiences, Redux', *Theatre Survey*, 47: 2 (November), pp. 225–230.

Brown, A. & Novak, J. (2007), *Assessing the Intrinsic Impacts of a Live Performance*, WolfBrown, http://www.wolfbrown.com/mups_downloads/Impact_Study_Final_Version_full.pdf. (accessed 24 March 2011).

Butsch, R. (2008), *The Citizen Audience: Crowds, Publics and Individuals*, New York and London: Routledge.

Fearon, F. (2010), 'Decoding the Audience: A Theoretical Paradigm for the Analysis of the "Real" Audience and their Creation of Meaning', *About Performance*, 10, pp. 119–135.

Freshwater, H. (2009), *Theatre and Audience*, London: Palgrave Macmillan.

Hennion, A., (2001), 'Music Lovers: Taste as Performance', *Theory, Culture and Society*, 18: 5, pp. 1–22.

Keaney, E. (2008), 'Understanding Arts Audiences: Existing Data and What it Tells Us', *Cultural Trends*, 17: 2, pp. 97–113.

Morley, D. (2006), 'Unanswered Questions in Audience Research', *The Communication Review*, 9: 2, pp. 101–121.

Pearson, R. & Messenger Davies, M. (2005), 'Class Acts? Public and Private Values and the Cultural Habits of Theatregoers', in S. Livingstone (ed.), *Audience and Publics: When Cultural Engagement Matters for the Public Sphere*, Bristol: Intellect.

Pitts, S. (2005), 'What Makes an Audience? Investigating the Roles and Experiences of Listeners at a Chamber Music Festival', *Music and Letters*, 86: 2, pp. 257–269.

Press, A. (2006), 'Audience Research in the Post-Audience Age: An Introduction to Barker and Morley', *Communication Review*, 9: 2, pp. 93–100.

Radbourne, J., Johanson, K., Glow, H. & White, T. (2009), 'The Audience Experience: Measuring Quality in the Performing Arts', *International Journal of Arts Management*, Spring 11: 3 pp. 16–29.

Ratsoy, G. (2008), 'Making an Exhibition of a Theatre Audience: Research through Photography', *Small Cities Imprint*, 1: 1, pp. 8–14.

Reason, M. (2004), 'Theatre Audiences and Perceptions of "Liveness" in Performance', *Participations*, 1: 2 (May).

——— (2010), *The Young Audience: Exploring and Enhancing Children's Experiences of Theatre*, Stoke on Trent: Trentham Books.

Sauter, W. (2002), 'Who Reacts When, How and upon What: From Audience Surveys to the Theatrical Event', *Contemporary Theatre Review*, 12: 3, pp. 115–129.

Schoenmakers, H. & Tulloch, J. (2004), 'From Audience Research to the Study of Theatrical Events: A Shift in Focus', in V. Cremona, P. Eversmann, H. van Maanen, W. Sauter & J. Tulloch (eds), *Theatrical Events: Borders, Dynamics and Frames*, New York: Rodopi.

Scollen, R. (2007), 'Theatre Talks Evolve into Talking Theatre', in Y. Feiler, R. Hoogland and K. Westerling (eds), *Willmar in the World: Young Scholars Exploring the Theatrical Event*, Stockholm: Stockholm University.

Vincs, K., Stevens, C. & Schubert, E. (2009), 'Measuring Responses to Dance: Is there a Grammar of Dance?', in *Dance Dialogues: Conversations Across Cultures, Artforms and Practices, Refereed Proceedings of the World Dance Alliance*, Global Summit, Brisbane, Australia, 13–18 July 2008, http://www.ausdance.org.au/resources/publications/dance-dialogues.html (accessed September 2011).

——— (2010), 'Effects of Observer Experience on Continuous Measures of Engagement with a Contemporary Dance Work', in W. Christensen, E. Schier, & J. Sutton (eds), *ASCS09: Proceedings of the 9th Conference of the Australasian Society for Cognitive Science*, Sydney: Macquarie Centre for Cognitive Science, pp. 357–361.

Walmsley, B. (2011), '"A Big Part of My Life": A Qualitative Study of the Impact of Theatre', AIMAC conference paper, Antwerp, July.

Zangwill, N. (1999), 'Art and Audience', *Journal of Aesthetics and Art Criticism*, 57: 3, pp. 315–332.

Index

Notes